GUINEA PIGLOPAEDIA

A Complete Guide To Guinea Pigs

Margaret Elward
& Mette Ruelokke

WITHDRAWN

RINGPRESS

Published by Ringpress Books,
A Division of Interpet Publishing
Vincent Lane, Dorking, Surrey RH4 3YX

ISBN 978 1 86054 251 0

Manufactured in Thailand supervised by
Kyodo Printing Singapore

10 9 8 7 6

CONTENTS

3

Uterine problems; Calluses; Bumble foot; Teeth; Scent glands; Sebaceous cysts; Red urine; Stomach impaction; Parasites; Injuries; Hot weather tips); Problem behaviour (Biting, Timidity).

SECTION II: HEALTH CARE AND PHYSIOLOGY

Chapter Seven: ANATOMY AND PHYSIOLOGY   62

Skeleton; Teeth; Digestive system (Faeces; Food transit time); Senses (Sight; Sound; Smell; Taste; Touch); Liver and kidneys; Respiratory system; Heart; Reproduction (Male; Female; Mating and fertilisation; Monitoring the pregnancy; Birth; Guinea pig babies).

Chapter Eight: A-Z OF GUINEA PIG DISEASES & HEALTH PROBLEMS   78

An alphabetical listing of the major conditions affecting guinea pigs, outlining signs, causes and treatment.

SECTION III: VARIETIES, BREEDING AND SHOWING

Chapter Nine: GUINEA PIG VARIETIES   125

Coat type (Smooth-haired cavies; Long-haired cavies; Special coats); Purebreed cavies (The show animal); The Self-Cavy (The Pink Eyed White; The Self-Black; The Self-Cream; The Pink Eyed Golden; The Self-Red; The Self-Chocolate; The Self-Beige; The Self-Lilac); The non-self varieties (The Abyssinian; The Agouti; The Argente; Bi-colours; Brindles; The Crested Guinea Pig; The Coronet; The Dutch; The Himalayan; The Peruvian; The Rex-coated Cavy; Roans and Dalmations; The Satin; The Sheltie; The Texel; The Smooth Tortoiseshell and White; Tri-colours); Rarer varieties (The Alpaca; The Harlequin; The Magpie; The Merino; The Ridgeback; The Sable; The Slate; Tans and Foxes).

5

SECTION I:
PRINCIPLES OF KEEPING GUINEA PIGS

CHAPTER 1

THE HISTORY OF THE GUINEA PIG

1. Origins
2. Going international
3. Comparative evolution

Guinea pigs are beautiful, bright, vocal animals. Their origins lie deep in South America, but their popularity as pets has spread far and wide. Indeed, they were introduced to this status long before any other small animals.

They are also known as the Domestic Cavy, pronounced Cay-vee. They are small rodents, belonging to the family Caviidae in the mammalian order Rodentia. This order includes rats, mice, hamsters and rabbits. It is believed that their ancestor was the *Cavia cutleri* or Restless Cavy, which can still be found in South America today.

There are various subspecies and it is possible that one of them, *Cavia aperea tschudii*, which can be found on both sides of the Andes range of mountains, is the fount from which the domestic guinea pig has sprung.

In the wild, cavies normally live in family groups among long grass, through which they make tunnels to move from one area to another. Although they are willing to use burrows that have been made by other animals and abandoned, they do not scrape out burrows of their own but live mainly on the surface.

They are shy animals, quite agile and easily scared. Baby cavies are born out in the open, and are much more advanced than other rodent babies. They have their eyes open, have all their hair and can move very quickly, which is just as well as they can be attacked by other

6

animals who are looking for food. The babies start eating solid food almost straight away, though they also suckle for about three weeks.

With domesticated guinea pigs, at this age the baby boars must be taken away from their mother or they will mate with her and any baby sows over a month old. The sows can be left with their mother permanently, or until she is again required for breeding.

1. ORIGINS

Cavies have been domesticated in South America for hundreds of years. The Incas kept them and fed them. Initially, they did not keep cavies as pets but killed them for food. As with the domestication of so many animals, it was practicality rather than sentiment which began that process. Humans realised that if the animals, which they had to go out and hunt in order to obtain food, were corralled in some way, they would save themselves a lot of time and effort.

This happened to rabbits, cows and sheep – and then selective breeding came in, because these animals provided clothing as well as food. Did the different coat colours and length of hair evolve as the first fashion statements by the wearers of such skins? It is doubtful whether guinea pig skins could have served any useful purpose in this regard, as the hairs fall out and the small skins were of no use as hides.

It seems that at one time the Incas had bred their cavies in several colours other than the agouti colouring found in the wild, but now it is only the white and brown colours that are found in the markets of South America where they are sometimes offered for sale.

Dogs and horses became domesticated because of their different skills – dogs as hunters, guardians and herders, and horses as a means of transport, carrying humans over vast distances at a speed much quicker than a man's gait.

Guinea pigs are still eaten in some South American countries today, but only on 'special occasions'. Unless a larger animal than is normally seen as a pet or on the show table has been bred, it is probably not a very sound economic proposition. Think of the time it would take to prepare guinea pigs for the table. It is not possible to prepare cavies in the same way as is done with rabbits, by skinning them. Cavies have hair like humans, not fur as rabbits do.

2. GOING INTERNATIONAL

Cavies were probably brought to Europe by Spanish

sailors returning from South America during the time of the great voyages of discovery in the 15th century. We know they arrived first in Spain and Portugal and, from there, spread throughout Europe. It is not certain whether the sailors kept them on board ships as pets, or if they bred them in order to augment their meagre food stocks. But, obviously, not all of them were eaten.

In the UK, cavies are usually known as guinea pigs. This name may have come partly from the Spanish name conchinillo or "little pig" (it is thought that when ready for the table they look like little pigs) but nobody seems to know where the 'guinea' comes from. Possibly they went from Guiana (a region in northern South America) with the Spanish sailors who transported them on ships travelling to Europe. Alternatively, when the animals first arrived in Europe, they were very expensive to buy, and this high value led to the word Guinea being attached to their name.

Cavies, or guinea pigs, are found over most of Europe as pets. Here is an old rhyme, which suggests cavies have been known under the name guinea pig for many years. It goes like this.
Why doesn't a guinea pig wag his tail?
'Cause he hasn't got a tail to wag!
All the other animals that you can find
Have got a little tail stuck somewhere on behind.
If they'd only put a tail on a guinea pig
And finished off a decent job
The price of a guinea pig would go right up
From a guinea to thirty bob!
(Many years ago the guinea was a coin worth £1.05 in today's money, and thirty bob was £1.50!)
Many people who keep cavies for exhibition and show refer to them as "guineas" or even "the pigs".

Today, guinea pigs are known in France as cochon d'Inde or cobaye, in German as meerschweinchen, in Spanish as cobayo and in Russian as morskaya swinya.

3. COMPARATIVE EVOLUTION

There are some guinea pig owners who consider that their animals bear a marked similarity to horses. They claim that the prehistoric horse is similar in appearance to the guinea pig.

At first glance, it seems rather silly to compare the animals. Just look at them. Today's horse is large and tall, long-legged, hoofed, muscular, sleek and powerful. Cavies are small and close to the ground with a rather humble, egg shape. On closer inspection, however, things get very interesting. Perhaps this is because both species evolved in a similar habitat, the grassy plain.

When species are exposed to similar environmental stresses, similar features are selected for convergent evolutionary results. For instance, although whales are mammals, penguins are birds, and fish are fish, they all have streamlined bodies and fins or flippers so that they can move through the water. Two unrelated plants, the African euphorbia and American cactus, both have a thick, fleshy shape with waxy skin and spines. These are adaptations to a desert climate in order to retain moisture and to keep animals from taking advantage of their precious store.

Horses and guinea pigs both evolved to avoid predators. They are both prey animals, not attackers. They ate, reproduced, and coped with the elements on the grassy plain. They evolved many adaptations to achieve these goals. These adaptations are similar in ways that helped them cope with the overall environment, but different where their needs varied.

Cavies and horses are social animals, preferring to live in herds. This adaptation provides more eyes, ears and noses to sense the approach of danger and to sound the alarm so that others can rest. This way, no one animal becomes exhausted by sentry duty. Also, when many animals flee together, it forms a confusing jumble of shapes, and a predator has a harder time focusing on a single individual to catch. In herds, young animals are better protected than if they were off by themselves.

Horses and guinea pig babies are born fully covered with hair, their eyes are open, and they are able to stand and run shortly after birth. This is because they must be able to stay with the herd in order to be safe.

Both horses and guinea pigs use flight to avoid predators, but they use it in different ways. A horse is able to outrun its enemies on the flat, it has a deadly kick, and can also bite, shake, throw and stomp its enemy. Guinea pigs are smaller and live down in the grasses. They combine flight with out-manoeuvring their enemies and taking cover. They are fast, agile and can turn without pause through memorised tracks of grass tunnels and along all the ups and downs of the terrain. They can wedge themselves into tiny cracks and crevices where they hide until it is safe to come out. At times, guinea pigs may lunge at a predator to hold off an attack but, even so, guinea pigs remain more vulnerable and have a shorter lifespan than horses, so they must make up for this by being capable of reproducing at an astounding rate, which they do. Both horses and guinea pigs have incisors for clipping mouthfuls of vegetation and molars for grinding, with a gap in between. The food that they eat is hard and coarse, which wears down their teeth. To compensate for this, horse teeth constantly erupt and cavy teeth constantly grow. Both are best adapted to food that is highly fibrous and of relatively low nutritional value (grass hay). Both animals, therefore, have a large caecum to help digest their food and can pass large amounts of partially digested food through their systems in order to get what they can from it and then move on to the next mouthful. As an aside, cows have a slightly different way of digesting. A cow must digest its food down to smaller particles before it can pass through its system. It does better on richer feed, such as alfalfa, and it regurgitates and re-chews its food (chews its cud) until the food can pass on through. A baby horse will eat manure to colonize its gut with beneficial bacteria. Guinea pigs eat their own droppings for beneficial vitamins.

An animal must manage its body temperature. A great deal of heat is lost through the skin. Two animals of the same shape but of different sizes will lose heat at different rates. The smaller one will lose heat more rapidly. This is because, shape being equal, the smaller animal has a larger surface-to-volume ratio. Since a sphere has the smallest surface-to-volume ratio of any other shape, small animals such as guinea pigs can reduce heat loss by having a more spherical body. Could guinea pigs have lost their tails in order to be more compact and to lose less heat? A horse's longer, thinner limbs aid in the necessary dissipation of its body's excess heat.

Another way for an animal to stay warm is to have a higher metabolic rate. A guinea pig has a faster heartbeat and eats more in relation to its weight than a horse. Perhaps the expression "eating like a horse" should read "eating like a guinea pig".

Horses buck and jump for joy in an almost popcorn-like manner (as do sheep and lambs) – and so do guinea pigs, kicking out with both their hind feet.

> *Owner observation: "The way I open my cavy's mouth so that he will take his medicine is exactly the same as opening a horse's mouth to get the bit in."*

CHAPTER 2

THE PET GUINEA PIG

1. Size
2. Sounds
3. Sociability
4. Sight
5. Handling
6. Classroom pets
7. Therapy pets
8. Lifespan
9. Recognising illness
10. Final parting

Guinea pigs make ideal pets and have a devoted legion of past and present owners. Being that much bigger than other small animals kept as pets, such as hamsters, they are much easier to catch if they do slip out of your hands. Although they will often make a dash for cover, they are not able to hide in the furniture, as can smaller animals such as mice and gerbils, although they can get into inconvenient places.

Although they are rodents and can gnaw, they are less likely to try to eat your furniture. However, you will need to keep an eye on them if they are allowed the freedom of a room. There are trained rabbits that are allowed such license, but cavies cannot be trained in this way.

They do not have to be taken for a walk like a dog, neither do they chase, toy with and then kill mice and birds as a cat does. They are not nocturnal and so do not sleep all day and keep you awake at night.

They can be safely left at home in a cage while you go off to work or school, and when you return they do appreciate affection and return it. They usually enjoy being handled and cuddled, and they will talk to you using a variety of squeaks, churrs and other sounds. You only have to rustle a bag and they will start calling to you although, possibly, this may be because they are hoping for treats!

Their most distinctive and appealing characteristic is what has

11

become known as 'popcorning'. They jump and leap, just like popcorn does when it is heated. Guinea pigs are not furry, cuddly toys; they respond to stimulation and interest.

They can also show their displeasure by giving a nasty nip. Then you have to ask yourself – did you do something wrong?

1. SIZE

Guinea pigs will never grow too large for children to handle.
- Newborn pigs are about 9.5 cm long (under 4 inches), but depending on the size of the litter can be as little as 8 cm (just over 3 inches).
- At five weeks old they are usually between 13-18 cm long (5-7 inches).
- At four months they are between 18-23 cm (7-9 inches) in length.
- A guinea pig is not fully grown until it reaches the age of 14 months, by which time it will be between 23-27 cm (9-10$\frac{1}{2}$ inches).

Adult male cavies normally now weigh between 1.1 kg-1.2 kg ($2\frac{1}{2}$-$2\frac{3}{4}$ lb) depending on the breed. Females weigh slightly less than full-grown boars. In recent times there had been an increase in breeding from under-age generations, and this has resulted in the decline of the average weight of the adult. Although a 1.8 kg (4 lb) guinea pig was sometimes seen in the past, a boar of 1.5 kg ($3\frac{1}{4}$ lb) will be remarked on at a show today.

2. SOUNDS

One of the most delightful aspects of guinea pig behaviour is their vocal ability. They have a range of grunts, squeaks or wheeks, coos, gurgles and chirrups. As you get to understand your pet, you will become more attuned to each sound.

The young guinea pig gives out high-pitched squeaks, which alert the mother to the fact that it wants attention. Adults will coo to each other, which resembles the human behaviour of murmuring sweet nothings in certain circumstances. Male adults will chatter their teeth at other male adults if a matter of hierarchy is being discussed.

Teeth-chattering is a sign of anger and the owner should be alert to this. Never put an unguarded hand in the cage or hutch when a guinea pig is chattering its teeth – with its poor eyesight, a pig might well bite

CASE HISTORY

"Harry always, and it really is always, whistles and wheeks when he hears the fridge door opening, or a bag being opened, or when he hears the sound of his owner walking into the room. His pal, Youp, sits beside him, totally quiet, but with an expression on his face that is saying 'You tell 'em Harry!'"

anything that touches it. If you must handle a pig at such a time, be sure to wear a sturdy glove.

All guinea pigs will squeal when frightened, and this is a sound you will hear if you are mishandling your pet, or if something external is troubling it. Or it may go totally silent, which is an even greater indication of fear. It is rather like paralysis. Your pig needs help immediately.

Some guinea pigs even sing. There are many breeders who have never heard this and it is indeed a strange phenomenon. It may be caused by the action of the teeth rubbing together in an unusual way. If you look closely during a bout of singing, it is possible to see the jaws of the guinea pig moving from

CASE HISTORY

"I was lying in my chair after dinner and holding Suzy on my chest. Her head was only a few inches from my face and, for whatever reason, I gave out a short whistle. Her ears twitched and I thought this was kind of cute so I did it a few more times. Each time I whistled she would twitch her ears. All of a sudden, she stuck her head up in the air and started to sing and chirp. This wasn't the usual guinea pig noises of squeaking, purring, chattering or anything like that; she was actually singing. It was a blend of high-pitched chirping along with a continuous and beautiful warbling. It was the most beautiful noise I have ever heard! She continued non-stop for about 30-40 seconds. I was absolutely transfixed by this outburst from her. I was frozen with awe and afraid to move or make a sound because I was scared I would interrupt her singing. My wife came into the living room where I was holding Suzy a few minutes later and I tried whistling again. She sang briefly, but only for a few seconds".

side to side rather than up and down as normal. What is certain is the effect a singing pig has on others in the cage or hutch: pure terror. The other pigs will rush around trying to hide from the strange sound, they will start shuddering and food will be ignored. It is advisable to remove a singing pig from a shared home until it has stopped its song.

3. SOCIABILITY

Guineas pigs are highly sociable characters. In the wild they lived in groups and domestication does not seem to have changed them very much. They retain all the characteristics of being prey animals; being surrounded by like-minded friends gives them a feeling of safety.

CASE HISTORY

Several guinea pigs live in the garden of a well-appointed apartment. The owner says that her great joy is going down to see them in the morning. "I am welcomed by their noisy wheeks and the smell of fresh hay. When I look in, I see clean cages and happy, healthy pigs, running around their cosy, but spacious, homes. When I tip new food into their feed bin, the chatter goes up all around the shed, as if they are telling each other that there is new food about and asking for their share. When I come down with a bag of carrots or other treats, they hear the bag and start up their wheeking and they don't stop until I give it to them."

4. SIGHT

What can guinea pigs actually see? This is a question that intrigues all pet owners of whatever species, be it cat, dog, horse or guinea pig, because animals seem to see things that we humans can't. You know, because you have had that feeling when your pet is looking hard at something totally invisible to you.

Because of the set of their eyes, guinea pigs can see what is in front of them and to the side of them without moving their eyes. This is typical of a prey animal that needs this wide field of vision.

Guinea pigs excel in smelling and hearing. They will know food is on the way because they can hear the owner's footsteps, but they are not able to see us until we are very near the hutch. When food is given they will identify it through smell rather than sight.

Some guinea pig owners notice that their animals seem fascinated by the television. Also, when in the kitchen with the window slightly open, they will gaze through it. If the window is closed, they don't bother. Is this because the glass then obstructs their angle of view, or is it that the slight breeze has been cut off?

What is generally agreed is that a guinea pig's range of vision may be as little as a metre. This may explain why they are sometimes seen to be uncomfortable and disorientated in hutches or pens that are too large: they worry if they cannot see to the other side, especially if they are young. If your guinea pig is experiencing this sort of 'agoraphobia', put a cardboard box on its side so that the pig has somewhere to hide.

5. HANDLING

Guinea pigs readily become used to being handled and they thrive on affection and company. The more they are handled in the correct way, the tamer they become.

To handle your guinea pig, guide it to the corner of its home then put your right hand around its shoulder. Slip your other hand underneath the pig to take the weight, then lift it up, allowing the back toes to go between the fingers of your left hand and the front legs to rest on your wrist. This way your guinea pig is secure and unlikely to become distressed – simply cuddled against the chest, the guinea pig can easily be dropped. All exhibition guinea pigs are handled in the way described above. If they are carried in any other way, they tend to feel insecure and spoil their coats by wriggling and crushing.

If the guinea pig is held as advised, there is usually little danger of the handler being scratched by sharp nails, but younger pigs can have their nails filed lightly with an emery board to reduce the sharpness. An older pig can have its nails trimmed with an ordinary nail clipper, but be sure to cut well away from the blood vessel, which appears as a thin red line in the nail.

One danger to watch out for, when you are cuddling your guinea pig on your lap, is that it might pee on you (see Toilet Training below). This does not seem to be an indication that the guinea pig does not want to be handled, or any sort of aggressive display; it just happens with some pigs. Take the precaution of covering yourself with a protective towel until the young guinea pig has been toilet trained.

TOILET TRAINING
Just as a child will rush off to the toilet, so a guinea pig being nursed
by a member of the family must be allowed to return to its box or
hutch after a while so that it can go to the toilet. This way it will not
pee on the child handler (which can be distressing) and will learn to go
in its box or hutch.

TEMPERAMENT
Guinea pigs are gorgeous, as everyone knows. However, they are not
toys and they can make their feelings known. As previously mentioned,
the chattering of teeth is a sign of anger, and it really does mean "leave
me alone".

JUMPING
There are various reports about how high a guinea pig can jump. What
is certain is that in Australia guinea pig races have been organised, and
these have featured jumps, as well as lanes, for the guinea pigs to run
in. Such steeplechases for guinea pigs tend to be frowned on elsewhere.

KICKING
Guinea pigs can kick. There was a male who, when excited, or when
cross with his female companion, would run past her and flip his legs
sideways at her in a very well-placed kick. He was a very placid, gentle
pig except when he got into this mood. Once, he kicked her and
knocked her back legs from under her.

One loving, suckling mother would kick her young when she had
tired of nursing them. They would scamper away and leave her alone
for a few minutes. She was actually a good mum, and would accept
the babies back after she had had a few minutes' peace and quiet.

Kicking is in the guinea pig's nature. When feeding them, you will
sometimes find that, when adding something extra, a pig will, without
looking, kick out with one leg like a horse.

When sows are resting together, and one walks by and knocks into
another, the sow that has been disturbed will sometimes dart its head
out like a snake and knock the other pig, as if to say "don't do that
again". Then they all go back to resting.

6. CLASSROOM PETS
Many people first come into contact with guinea pigs
in the classic schoolroom situation. Live animals are
kept there almost as an extension of the nature table.

16

Opinions vary as to whether this is good or bad, for the guinea pig, for the children and for the teachers. Of course each situation varies, in a school as well as in a home. There are loving classroom environments and inappropriate ones, just as there are people keeping guinea pigs in their home in a tiny cage that they rarely clean.

In the best classrooms, the guinea pigs are watched by the children, fed by them and play time is with one child at a time, inside a large pen with the child sitting down at all times and always supervised by a teacher. The guinea pigs are also taken home by the teacher or children every weekend so they have their own home to go to.

Older children can get involved with projects such as designing the ideal cage or enclosure for the guinea pig. They are encouraged to read about the animal's needs and do a budget on the cost of keeping a pet. Local experts, such as a vet and an animal welfare consultant, can be called in to comment on what the children have achieved. Teachers who have used this method feel that the most important aspect was the understanding the children acquired about the responsibility of owning a pet. They were taught to be caring and compassionate.

However, there are rules that must be observed if a pet is to be taken into a classroom.

- The teacher must take absolute and sole responsibility for the welfare of the guinea pig.
- It is now the rule, not the exception, that schools require a health certificate from a vet on each pet that comes into a classroom, each year. This means that the animal has to be seen by a vet every 12 months.
- The housing for that animal must be kept in perfect condition, so that children with allergies are not bothered by dust, pet dander or pet hair.

Opponents of having guinea pigs in classrooms raise many valid points. They feel that the guinea pig will be isolated and become confused through having so many handlers, but no real friends. Remember that the social group is very important to a guinea pig. It will be shunted from child to child during the day, and from emergency home to emergency home at weekends and during the holidays. And it will be left by itself every night.

There is also the objection to using animals in order to teach a child a sense of responsibility. Children, and a lot of adults, can become bored with the responsibility of looking after a pet. In this situation, the humans don't suffer, but the animal does.

So, unless you can really care for a guinea pig exposed to this sort of spotlight, don't even consider it.

7. THERAPY PETS

There is a school of thought that considers that all animals can be used as therapy pets. This is unwise in the case of small, fragile, prey animals such as guinea pigs, and harm has been done to them when they have been used in the wrong circumstances. Dogs are the best therapy pets. However, case histories can always prove the opposite. Guinea pigs have been taken into specialist children's hospitals and proved to be of great help.

One adolescent child had severe emotional and relationship problems and was unable to communicate. It was suggested that she be given a guinea pig to look after. Yes, it was a risk, but it worked. She started talking to the pet, looking after it, caring for it. In a matter of weeks she was communicating with her therapist.

The key point is that the pet, as well as the patient, has to be monitored, to make sure that everyone is truly in safe hands.

8. LIFESPAN

The average lifespan is in the region of seven years, though it is not unusual for guinea pigs to live several years longer. However, some die at a much younger age. The typical guinea pig lifespan is considerably longer than many small pets, and you should consider the commitment of daily feeding and regular cage cleaning before you decide to go ahead. You will also need to be able to make arrangements with a responsible friend or neighbour to look after your pets when you go on holiday. Always give written instructions as to how the guinea pigs are to be fed etc. and have a trial run prior to going away. Mistakes can be made by giving too little or too much food. Remember to remind the temporary keeper to keep the hutch or cage door shut after each feeding time.

9. RECOGNISING ILLNESS

Guinea pig illnesses will be discussed in detail later in this book, but you must be aware, as an owner, that these are prey animals who will conceal their weaknesses.

If your guinea pig is ill, it won't tell you. You have to be aware of its moods and behaviour and understand when it appears to be off-colour.

10. FINAL PARTING

It is always upsetting when a loved pet dies. You do your best for them when you know they are ill, and sometimes you have to make the decision to have them put to sleep. But, while you are grieving, remember that animals can grieve as well. Guinea pigs are sociable creatures and will miss a departed companion. The death of a guinea pig is felt by all in a stud; there is a quietness and the others know that something has happened. Some guinea pigs can become quite ill when they lose a companion. You have to deal with it, and decide what is the best course of action for your living guinea pig pets that are feeling sad about the death.

CASE HISTORY

When Cinnamon passed away, it was quiet and gentle. She was four-and-a-half years old. She was suffering from a few ailments but remained as fussy and cantankerous as ever, always slamming her cagemate, Pepper, out of the way if a treat was on offer. Even on her last day, she came for her treat, even though she was not able to eat it. She was held gently by her owner, from time to time, during that period. When she was in the guinea pigs' housing, Pepper lay beside her. The end had come when Pepper was seen lying at the other end of the cage away from her.

CHAPTER 3

CHOOSING A GUINEA PIG

1. Where to go
2. Making your choice
3. How many?
4. Quarantine
5. Guineas and other animals
6. The homecoming

Many people think they would like to start with a baby guinea pig. They are very agile but can be trained very quickly if held correctly from the outset (see Handling, page 15).

1. WHERE TO GO

Friends: You can often obtain your first guinea pig from a friend or neighbour whose own pet has had babies, or you can buy straight from a fancier who has some for sale.

Clubs: Most cavy clubs or societies hold shows, which are open to the public. Here you would not only be able to see many of the varieties of cavy but you would also be able to meet fanciers and, in most cases, be able to choose your cavies in the 'for sale stock' section. There will be smooth-coated, rough-haired and long-haired varieties. A leaflet is given to first-time buyers telling them how to care for their guinea pig.

Breeders: There are cavy specialists who just love to see little guinea pigs and love taking care of them. They are the ones who sell their spare breeding stock to any interested fancier. This is how the various varieties increase in popularity and how the clubs increase their memberships. This type of fancier/breeder will not usually look to make much money from the sale of cavies, and this is often the way to get good-quality guinea pigs at very reasonable prices.

There are some breeders who do it strictly for the money. Beware, because often the guinea pigs produced from such an environment may look good but have not been well kept. They may be of nice, or even rare, colour but they have come from over-bred stock. Sometimes females are sold off because they have exhausted themselves as potential breeding material. Do not buy stock aged over 18 months to two years.

Pet shops: Many pet shops sell guinea pigs. However, there can be pitfalls buying from some shops. Often, the cavies are sold too young. Eight weeks old is the youngest age at which a baby guinea pig should be sold. Before this age, the stress of the move from home to shop, and then shop to new home, can be too much and the little animal becomes very stressed. Also, many pet shops are not staffed by people who know how to sex cavies, and it is not unusual for people to buy female cavies from a shop and find that they are already pregnant. As these animals are usually young, this is also not a good thing. If you are buying from a pet shop, take somebody with you who knows how to sex the animals. This can also be a more expensive way of buying your cavies.

Rescue centres: It is also often possible now to buy guinea pigs from rescue centres – either specialist small-animal centres or from the more usual city ones. These will usually have staff who are able to ensure that the animals are in good health and, as they often have slightly older guinea pigs, they could have just what you are looking for. The internet is also a great place for discovering caring guinea pigs owners who really need to find homes for abandoned pigs that they have discovered. You can also talk to other owners on the websites.

A TALE OF TWO RESCUES
Twinkle was rescued from an unscrupulous pet store, when he was seen floundering in the middle of about 20 other guinea pigs. He looked more like a rat, with ribs sticking out, all hipbones and ears. He was obviously the runt of one of the litters in the pen, and was being chased by the other pigs. At the time, he couldn't have been more than a week old. His rescuers took him home and fed him on a mash of

pellets, watered milk, honey and vitamins. He didn't know how to eat on his own, so he was hand-fed. And he snuggled up to his owner all the time. Thinking that Twinkle would be happier with a companion, the owners went to a rescue pound and found Charlie, who was full of personality – and, as it turned out, lice. Anyway, Charlie was cured of his lice, and the two guinea pigs were put in the same cage but separated by a wire net. They loved it. Charlie had obviously been on his own all his life, and Twinkle had never learned guinea pig behaviour. When the time was right, the wire was removed and they lived together, each learning from the other. It was a total success story.

2. MAKING YOUR CHOICE

The most important consideration is to buy a healthy guinea pig. So how do you recognise one?

- Watch it for a while. Does it run around actively? Does it sit up normally, without hunching its back? If it points its head upwards and moves around in circles, it is likely to be blind.
- Do the cage droppings look normal? They should be thin and rounded, rather like a bean. Any hint of loose motions, and you should be suspicious about the conditions in which the animal is being kept. Loose motions at any time during a guinea pig's life indicates that it has a health problem about which advice should be sought.
- The hair should be bright, with no hint of a scurfy skin beneath, and no loss of hair. Bald patches indicate skin infections or infestations of parasites. Spray with a mite spray used for pet birds.
- You must handle the guinea pig you are thinking of acquiring. Do this gently and carefully, holding its body in one hand while you support its backside in the other. Let its spine lean against the palm of your hand.
- Do not be put off if the animal is shy. How would you react if you were, literally, picked up by a stranger? But does it feel pleasantly rounded, or is it rather thin or a little bit flabby? If it is thin and limp, you should not take it.
- Look into its eyes. Are they bright and slightly moist? That is good. If they are moist to runny, that is bad.
- If you see any crusty deposits around the eyes or mouth, be very wary. You should not buy if you see these deposits.
- Very, very gently have a look at the guinea pig's mouth. Make sure you are supporting its whole body, and then prise open the mouth

with your little finger. You are looking to see if the two incisor teeth and the molars of the upper jaw just touch those of the lower jaw. If they do, then this is good. It means that the teeth will wear naturally. If they don't, then this little animal will have problems in later life, which can lead to euthanasia.
• Check its feet. Do they look pink and healthy or are there signs of inflammation? What is the condition of the claws? Are they growing straight, or at an angle?

And, remember, there is always a great temptation to feel sorry for the runt of any litter, the neglected animal in the pet shop, the waif and stray. Think very carefully when letting your heart rule your head. Can you cope with the complications? We would all like to save the world. Just consider what you are doing when you purchase a pet. After all, you are that pet's whole world.

3. HOW MANY?

Before you consider obtaining a guinea pig, you should work out how many you want. These are sociable animals and, in the wild, would live in colonies; therefore it is not a good idea to keep one on its own. However, some cavies prefer to be kept singly; it depends on the individual. But you must remember, whatever the experts tell you, animals are individuals and they may display some very unexpected reactions to your best-laid plans.

Unless you want to breed your pets, you should keep animals of the same sex together. Two boars or two sows will usually live happily together. It can often be difficult asking two older animals to cohabit, but most males and females will accept a youngster. If you are buying your first cavies then, providing they have been purchased at the same time, they will usually settle down together without any trouble if they are young ones.

Most guinea pigs like to share a hutch, but you could provide two separate places in the hutch for them to go in (for example, two cardboard boxes). As long as the cage is big enough, there shouldn't be too much of a problem keeping them together.

If you are putting a young male in with an older female, it is advisable to have the male neutered, which is a simple operation in the hands of a good veterinarian.

AN OWNER'S VERDICT
Spaying guinea pigs is quite a difficult operation but neutering

(castrating a male) is pretty run-of-the-mill. Both operations have to be done by experienced cavy vets so that the anaesthetic and antibiotics are correct.

Most of our pigs have been spayed and neutered because we get them from shelters and it has already been done, or we have it done so they can live together more peacefully. There are currently three herds in the same room, and all those hormones can occasionally lead to fighting.

Males together: Some males get on fine when introduced to other males, but a lot will not get on. When you introduce two boys, they will start rumbling at each other and will try to mount each other. They are not trying to mate when they do this; they are trying to establish dominance. This is normal. However, if they start attacking each other, you should separate them. Even neutered males can fight, but it might just be a personality clash. The best pairing of males is two who have been raised together and who have had no contact with females.

Male and female: If you get a girl, when you introduce her to the male there will again be the rumbling and mounting behaviour as the male tries to mate her. If the sow is not in season, she will reject his advances and become slightly aggressive with him. If she is in season, she will usually be submissive to him.

One of the most delightful pairings is that of a mature neutered boar who wants company and a female who does not want to be harassed. But this can produce an unexpected result. Do not put the two together until some time has elapsed after the male has been neutered. It seems that the boar can still retain latent but active sperm.

Two females: These generally get on very well. Basically, put the girls together and let them work it out. It sounds scary but, if supervised properly and provided with a 'bolt-hole' (a little wooden den in case they need to get away from things), they should be fine. But there are always exceptions.

There was no reason why Poppy and Coco should not get on but Poppy just did not like Coco. She would launch and snap at poor Coco and pee on her too, which was very sad because Coco wanted to be friends with Poppy and she would run to her whenever she was scared. Funnily enough, when it suited her, Poppy would guard Coco and be protective of her.

CASE HISTORY

Smudge was a gorgeous, mainly white Abby, with big black and brown smudges on his face, but he was just not satisfied with his owners lavishing attention on him and it became clear that he wanted a piggie friend – not just two silly big humans. The owner searched for advice and it was suggested that they either got a very young baby boy (but there was no guarantee that two boys would get along once baby had grown up) or get Smudge neutered and then buy him a girl pal. That is what they decided to do and it was the best thing for him. His personality changed overnight once he met Poppy, a tiny little brown thing that looked a bit like a dinosaur because she had a big spiky bit of hair that ran all along the top of her back [Ridgeback]. The two pigs were put in cages side by side and let out at different times so that they could investigate each other in safety. When they were eventually introduced about a month later, they were so happy to see each other. And so were the owners when Poppy subsequently produced young, the result of the latent sperm syndrome.

4. QUARANTINE

If you are adding a new guinea pig to your existing tribe, there is a school of thought which considers that you should keep it in quarantine for at least three weeks in order to make sure that it does not have any illnesses that could be transmitted. After this, give the newcomer a cage next to its cagemate-to-be for another few days, so that they can get used to each other and each other's smell through the safety of cage bars before actually meeting face to face. With sows, you can probably then put them together, having introduced them during floor time. With boys you can begin introducing them during floor time, but make sure it is on neutral territory to avoid major conflict!

The other idea is that a new young guinea pig, if it has been acquired from a reputable breeder so that it is definitely clean and cared for, should be introduced to its future companions immediately. The way to do this is to rub the newcomer with some soiled bedding from the incumbents and then pop it in the cage. This is because young guinea pigs will pine if left alone and can die. If this rapid introduction looks like causing trouble, then get another young guinea pig and put the two little ones in together.

5. GUINEAS AND OTHER ANIMALS

It is not a good idea to keep rabbits and cavies together. There are several reasons for this, two of the most important being that they require different diets; the rabbit does not need the inclusion of vitamin C and eats slightly different food. Also, the rabbit is usually bigger than the cavy, it has very powerful hind legs, and can easily hurt a cavy should it get in the way when the rabbit bounces around the cage, especially if the rabbit has been frightened by something. A doe rabbit when in season is aggressive and will bite and hurt a guinea pig.

Be very careful about leaving your guinea pigs alone with your dogs. One hot day, a guinea pig owner had left her three pigs in their run in the garden with secure wire around it. The back door was open so her two dogs could come and go as they pleased. The dogs were used to living with other animals. She was working inside. Then some instinct made her go and check. The younger dog had broken through the wire and killed a young Sheltie by shaking it. Meanwhile, the other dog had gone into the run and was protecting the other two guinea pigs. There seemed to be no reason why a gentle dog, used to living with smaller creatures, should suddenly do this. It was also intriguing that the other dog showed all its guarding instincts towards the other two pigs and against its dog companion.

6. THE HOMECOMING

THE CARRIER

You do not need any special box or carrier to transport your new pet. A cardboard box, about the size used in supermarkets for six bottles of wine, is ideal for one older cavy or two youngsters.

Make sure the bottom of the box is securely taped up, and place some folded newspaper, about one inch of shavings, a small amount of hay and perhaps a piece of carrot inside. Make a few air holes near the top of the box and make sure that you are able to shut the top flaps.

Do not allow anyone to carry the cavy in their arms, whether you are walking or travelling by bus or car, and keep the box closed until you get home. If the animal did try to escape, it could fall and damage itself or get injured. Be safe, not sorry.

Remember that traffic noise and people passing by are all alien sounds to a cavy who has only been used to his own cage and his breeders.

ARRIVING HOME

When you reach home and you have the cage all ready, lift the cavy out of the box and give it a cuddle. At first it may appear nervous and scrabble a bit, but this is because everything is new to it in your house or garden. After a few minutes, place it in the cage you have prepared for it and shut the door. Talk to it so that it begins to know your voice.

SETTLING IN

Do not pass the guinea pig from person to person for the first few days. Let one person hold and cuddle it for a few minutes and then let it rest for a couple of hours in its new home before it is handled by someone else, so that it has time to get to know your scents and start feeling safe. After a few days, it will have become used to you and be quite at home. Remember, it also has to get used to the cage as well and it does need a little bit of patience. Think how you would feel in a new house or even a new school. However, please do not put the cavy in the cage and leave it for a week or so to settle down. Yes, it will get used to the cage but it may then become harder to catch, as it does not know you and will try to hide from you. Handle it gently two or three times a day if possible at first, so that it gets to know you. After a couple of weeks or sometimes just a few days, you will find the cavy coming to the front of the cage to welcome you when you visit.

When you want to catch your cavy, please don't grab it by the scruff of its neck. Grabbing it from above and holding and squeezing its ribs can cause serious damage to the rib cage or to internal organs. The lower part of the body is particularly vulnerable and a guinea pig should never be grabbed below the rib cage. Children who do not realise this have, in the past, been responsible for causing injury and even death to a beloved pet because of faulty handling such as this. You should try to slide one hand under the tummy and rest the other on the top of the back. If your pig is very skittish, it can help to place one hand against the side of the cage near the back, using the other hand to guide the animal against it, and then slide one hand underneath. Do this in a quiet way and soon you will have no trouble catching your cavy. It is often better for an adult to catch the cavy initially and then pass it to a child.

If the guinea pig is dropped, look to see if it has broken any teeth. Being a rodent, they will grow again but root food must be cut up in small pieces so that it can pick it up with its lips and pass it back to the grinding teeth. Green food should be cut up with scissors. Any time a guinea pig stops eating its food, look to see if its teeth are broken.

CHAPTER 4

HOUSING YOUR CAVY

1. The hutch
2. Location
3. Size
4. Bedding
5. The run
6. Feeding bowls

It is advisable to have everything ready before you go to fetch your new pet, including a few days' supply of dry food and hay. Most responsible breeders will be able to tell you what food the guinea pig is used to and will often be willing to supply you with enough to enable you to change it to your diet, if you so wish, gradually.

The first and most important piece of equipment you will need is a hutch for your guinea pig. The main priorities for all animals are shelter and food. If your pet is to be housed in the garden, the hutch will need to be sturdy and weatherproofed. This will not be quite so important if the cage is to be kept in a shed or outhouse.

1. THE HUTCH

Hutches are normally made of wood. The strongest types of cage usually use good-quality tongue-and-groove timber for the sides and back. However, exterior-grade plywood is also a suitable material and this is probably the best material to use for the cage floor, as there will be no joints for the guinea pig to catch its nails in.

The cage should be treated with preservative inside and out, but make sure that the product you use is suitable for animals. If the cage

28

is to be permanently in a shed, or in something similar, then it will not need to be as weatherproof, but will still need to be treated with preservative to ensure protection for the wood from the ammonia in the guinea pigs' urine and droppings.

However, do not be tempted to use thin wood for the sides and back – even if the hutch is to be situated in a shed – as rats can gnaw through this.

FLOORING

The cages used for some other animals have a mesh floor; this is not advisable for cavies, as their feet are not covered with hair and it would be very uncomfortable for them. Also, their legs and feet are small and they could get caught in the wire and break when they tried to move. Guinea pigs should never stand on mesh or grids; the danger to their feet is tremendous. One of the worst abuses, that in the past commonly happened at shelters, is putting pigs in rabbit hutches with wire-grid flooring. Guineas can lose a leg, or even their life, that way.

The cage must not be allowed to sit on the ground, as this will make it rot. It either needs to have sturdy legs fitted, or it should be placed on a table. It must be made safe, to protect the guinea pigs from the attentions of predators. The ideal solution is to have the cage roughly 30 inches off the ground, as this makes it much easier for cleaning out and the day-to-day care of your cavies.

LIGHT AND AIR

The front of the cage should have a door with a wooden frame containing a wire mesh in order to allow light and air into the cage. This door usually covers about two-thirds of the front, with a smaller door of wood covering the rest of the front. This gives the owner easy access for feeding and cleaning out.

It can be a good idea to make a mesh frame that can be placed behind any windows in the hutch, to keep out cats and other predators. Also, in summer, it can be useful to also have one for the door so that a flow of air can move through the shed.

SLEEPING AREA

It is not necessary to provide guinea pigs with a sleeping compartment, as they do not make nests; however, the darkness provided by the solid section of the door will make an area that will provide them with a more restful space. And they do need bedding of hay or soft straw.

SECURITY
Some cages are fitted with a solid wooden panel, the same size as the front mesh opening, which can be fastened up over the front of the cage at night or in especially bad weather. If this is fitted, do please drill a few air holes in the flap, or have it slightly shorter than the height of the cage, so that air can get in. This also adds to security.

DOORS
The door needs to be strongly made and to have a strong fastener if the cage is to be situated outside. It is not that guinea pigs will force their way out – it is to prevent unwanted visitors from getting in. Even in urban areas, foxes and badgers do enter gardens, as do other people's cats and dogs. And rats kill guinea pigs. Some of these animals are very strong and can easily try to force a cage door open. Fit the cage door with a strong bolt and, if necessary, also secure it with a padlock. You should keep a careful watch for any attack by rats. They will gnaw through the backs of hutches, attack adult guinea pigs and kill them. Any babies will be torn to pieces and partially eaten.

ROOFING
The roof should slope, and be higher at the front than at the back. If the cage is to be kept outside, the roof should overhang all sides. The roof, sides and back should be covered with two or three layers of good-quality roofing felt to make certain that the inside will keep warm and dry. It can be a good idea to allow the roof a generous overhang at the front of the cage to allow you some protection when tending your cavies in bad weather.

2. LOCATION
The siting of the cage is important. Cavies are happiest in temperatures similar to those that humans find comfortable. They must have plenty of bedding. They are unable to stand getting wet and cold, and can easily catch pneumonia if they are left like this. For this reason, the cage must be sited so that it faces away from the prevailing wind so that the rain does not get blown into the cage. Cavies do not like very cold weather or excessive heat in the summer – both are potential killers.

WINTER QUARTERS
It is not necessary for the cage to be indoors, although if it is possible to move the cage into a shed or conservatory for the winter months,

that would be ideal. If the cage is outside and the weather is very cold and frosty, it is a good idea to hang an old carpet or something similar over the front as a little piece of protection from the cold. Do not use plastic to cover the front as this leads to condensation – the bedding will become very wet and the cavies will get chilled.

However, please let your cavies have some daylight and fresh air each day. Remember, the guinea pigs do not need extra heating in winter in the UK. If they have dry quarters and sufficient bedding, their coats will get thicker to provide extra warmth, but they will certainly suffer if they become too hot in the summer. Their hair is actually very warm, and, even if the top feels cold to the touch, if you burrow down to the skin, the temperature can feel very comfortable. Guinea pigs are actually more susceptible to draughts than cold, as humans can also be. You know how uncomfortable it can be when there is a draught in your sitting room.

THE SUMMER MONTHS

Guinea pigs are unable to perspire and are susceptible to heat stroke if left out in the sun or if they become too hot. Therefore, during the summer months, the cage should not be in a conservatory or sunroom; nor should the sun pour directly into the cage all day. If possible, move it to a shady corner of the garden when the weather is really sunny and warm. A greenhouse should never be used – summer or winter.

If your cage is in a shed, please make sure that it is possible to have the window open during the day and possibly at night as well in hot weather.

3. SIZE

The size of the cage will depend on the number of guinea pigs you are keeping in it. For two guinea pigs, a hutch or cage 62 cms x 38 cms x 38 cms (2 feet x 15 inches x 15 inches) gives them ample room. They never feel safe in a hutch or run that is large owing to their poor eyesight.

4. BEDDING

Wood chips are a bad idea. Most have wood oils that are toxic to guinea pigs. Even lighter woods are bad, as they are rough and hard and can hurt guinea pig feet. The best bedding is plain black-and-white newspaper. Line the cage with that.

Next add a pile of hay – you can never give too much hay. Guinea pigs do not overeat hay. If they have leftovers, they like to sleep in it.

31

And the newspaper under everything makes it easy to clean up; just roll it up and throw it away. Thick newspaper in the hutches holds the heat in winter so the guinea pigs are kept warm.

5. THE RUN

If you have a lawn in summer, it would be a good idea to create a run in which you can place the guinea pigs during the day to allow them to get some exercise and fresh air. This should be made using wire mesh fixed to a wooden frame. The size would depend on the size of your garden but a run 1.2 metres (4 ft) by 1.2 metres (4 ft) by about 30 cm (1 ft) high would give the guinea pigs plenty of space and give them grass to eat. To make the most of the available grass and also to prevent a build-up of droppings in any one area, the cage should be light enough to be easily moved. Remember that large garden pens can make guinea pigs wild – they can become frightened. So always put a cardboard box into the run so that they have somewhere to hide.

At one end of the run, a shelter should be provided, so that the guinea pigs can get out of the sun. It also gives them protection from the odd shower and somewhere to hide if they want to. The top of the run will need to be hinged so that you can gain access, but should also have secure fastenings to protect against it being opened accidentally. It would not be a good idea to leave the guinea pigs in the run at night for security reasons – and it might frighten them.

It is not a good idea to let your cavies run around your garden by themselves, as they will probably eat all your prize plants and could try some that are poisonous to them. Also, they could easily escape through small holes in the fence and could be chased by other animals.

6. FEEDING BOWLS

You will also need to have a bowl for dry food. Ideally, this should be fairly heavy so that the cavy does not tip it up when looking for its favourite morsel! It also needs to be easily washed. The earthenware dishes made for small dogs and cats are about the right size for one or two cavies. A heavy feeding bowl is especially important for a mother and her litter, as she can unwittingly trap a baby by overturning a bowl on top of it. At night it is sometimes better to take the bowl out altogether and leave some dried food on the floor of the home – a baby that has been trapped under a feeding bowl all night will usually be dead by the morning.

The cavy also needs water to drink. The best method of supplying this is in a bottle with an angled spout. The spout should be made of stainless steel so that it cannot be chewed. The bottle can be hung on the outside of the mesh front of the cage, by means of the wire supplied, and the spout protrudes into the cage. You can use a separate dish for water but it usually gets tipped up in the cage, making the bedding wet and soggy. The dish can also become full of bedding and droppings, so should not be used.

CASE HISTORY

One cavy owner lives in a desert region where most of the time the temperature is too high outdoors for guinea pigs. But there is a period in the year when it gets cooler, and so she lets them out. The yard is totally pig-proof so that they cannot get out. She places a large box, with tunnel holes in all its four sides, on the grass near some bushes. The pigs love rushing from the box into the bushes and back again. But they are never left unsupervised.

CHAPTER 5

FEEDING YOUR CAVY

1. Water
2. Dry food
3. Vegetables
4. Hay
5. Vitamin C
6. Grass
7. Wild food
8. A balanced diet

Cavies are herbivores, which means they are vegetarians; they do not eat meat in any form. In the wild, they would eat grass, herbs and weeds, including the seeds from grasses. They also eat fruit and vegetables that are growing wild. Do not let them near chocolate. This is poisonous for them.

Pet guinea pigs are great ones for developing exotic tastes. Owners have reported a variety of addictions, including garlic bread, curried rice, frozen lollipops and even cod roe spaghetti. Be very careful about feeding human treats. You might like them, and the guinea pig will look very cute eating them – possibly having stolen them from you with your connivance, but you could be doing your pet great harm. Stick to the proper guinea pig diet. If you don't, you could end up with a very obese animal, medical problems and a huge vet bill.

A great mistake is to let your guinea pig on to the table where you have been eating. This blurs the lines between owner and pet. Would you eat guinea pig food? Would it be good for you? Think what you are doing when you let your pig snack from your food.

1. WATER
This must be provided at all times, even though the animals gain water from the fresh foods in their diet.

34

Ideally, use a water bottle with a stainless steel tube, so that the cavies cannot chew through it. The water must be changed often and the water bottle cleaned regularly. The bottle is clipped on to the wire mesh of the cage, hutch or run.

If you need to feed a supplement of soluble vitamin C, this can be put into the water.

2. DRY FOOD

This may be a proprietary guinea pig food, but it is not always necessary to buy something special. Oats, bran, rolled barley, crushed cooked peas, flaked maize, soya-bean meal, grass pellets and similar can be mixed together and fed. Crushed lotus beans and linseed oil cake can be added.

Do not overfeed dry food. Give sufficient, but encourage the animals to eat it all. Do not feed so much that they can become selective and only eat certain foods. It is a good idea to give one type of food in the morning, perhaps the fresh food, and then the dry food in the evening.

If you also have other livestock, it may be possible for you to use the same food for your cavies. Proprietary goat mixes and coarse horse mix are both suitable for use as a dry food. Sugar beet cubes can be soaked in water and then mixed with bran and fed as part of the rations.

One definite prohibition is whole sunflower seeds. Guinea pigs love them but some will eat them to the exclusion of other food, which can cause deficiencies in the diet. Also, the husk can become trapped between the front teeth and cut into the roof of the mouth. This then has to be removed because, if left for any length of time, the pig will be very uncomfortable. Mixes including crushed sunflower seeds, or ones with the husk removed, are fine and the oil contained in the seeds is beneficial to the guinea pig's coat.

3. VEGETABLES

Hard vegetables are good for the teeth and are an important source of minerals and vitamins. Green vegetables are a source of vitamin C. The basic good vegetables are carrots, apples, green cabbage and dandelion leaves. Some guinea pigs like the more adventurous tastes of pears, tomatoes, broccoli and cauliflower leaves. Only give a quarter of an apple to each cavy, as the acid content can cause sores around the mouth.

4. HAY

This is essential to the diet as it aids digestion. Without

35

hay, the cavy will become ill. The hay must be of good quality, clean and, if possible, should be meadow hay. This should be at least three months old before giving it to the guinea pigs, but can still have a green tinge to it. Do not accept hay if it does not smell sweet or if it looks dusty or mouldy, as it will make the animals ill.

> **OWNER'S TIP**
>
> *There can be hazards with hay. A piece of hay can get stuck into the eye, right through to the cornea, or get under the eyelid. Vigilance is needed to ensure that hay is not causing any injuries. Have some eye-drops and some tear ointment to hand in case of emergencies.*

If you have some clean, dry storage space, it is much better to buy your hay from a farm that specialises in good-quality hay and can supply you with a bale at a time. Hay also makes a soft bed for the cavy, keeping it warm in the winter and helping to keep out the draughts.

Alternatively, you can buy cubed hay, which is possibly safer but may not have the same nutritional value. Several types of hay have been recommended by guinea pig owners over the years, alfalfa and timothy are just two of them, but, realistically, what is available depends on where you live. The best advice is to find the most reliable supplier and to discover for yourself what suits your guinea pigs.

It is a good idea to give hay later in the day, although it does not make a great deal of difference. Often, if you feed fresh food and hay together, some of the fresh food gets wasted under the hay.

5. VITAMIN C

Guinea pigs have a particular characteristic that makes them different from all other rodents and most other animals, but is one they share with humans. They are unable to manufacture their own vitamin C, which is essential to their diet. Without vitamin C, cavies can suffer problems with their immune system and also develop bone deformities similar to rickets in humans. Therefore, they need a diet that contains this vitamin in one form or another.

Where possible, vitamins and minerals should be provided by a daily supply of root and green foods. Many proprietary guinea pig foods have added vitamin C, but it is better that this should be not be relied on as the sole source. Anyway, feeding fresh food adds variety to the diet and gives the cavy an interest.

Foods rich in vitamin C should be fed daily. It is best to use a variety of foods, but no onions, leeks, garlic or anything else that grows from a bulb. Neither should you feed raw potato or rhubarb, nor the leaves from potato or rhubarb.

You should ensure that the food is fresh and, in the winter, make sure it has not been frozen, as it then becomes a soggy mess when it thaws out.

VEGETABLES
- Artichokes and their leaves
- Beetroot
- Broccoli
- Cabbage
- Carrots
- Cauliflower (especially the green leaves and stem)
- Celeriac
- Celery
- Chicory leaves
- Cucumber
- Fodder beet
- Green beans (and the bean plants if you have your own)
- Kale
- Kohlrabi
- Lettuce (especially green, leafy types, but not too much as it contains laudanum, which is a sedative)
- Mangel-wurzel
- Parsley
- Peas
- Spinach
- Swede (although not liked by the majority of guinea pigs)
- Sweetcorn
- Sweet peppers
- Turnip
- Tomato
- Young shoots of apple and pear trees.

FRUITS
- Apple
- Banana
- Kiwi fruit
- Pear

- Melon
- Strawberries and raspberries
- Guinea pigs have also been known to like oranges.

6. GRASS

This is a good source of vitamin C during the spring and summer; however, in winter, it contains very little. When it is possible to get fresh grass, it should be fed daily. If you go collecting it, make sure that it has not been sprayed with herbicide, which would be poisonous, and that it has not been contaminated by dogs or rats. Also, do not pick so much that it starts to heat up, as it can then harm the cavies.

> *Word of warning: Spinach, kale and parsley are very high in oxalic acid. This binds up with free-roaming calcium in the system and actually prevents the calcium from being absorbed. Instead, it collects in the bladder and kidneys, where it can form stones. Don't feed to excess.*

If you have a lawn, you could put the cavies out on it in a run. They will eat the grass and save you mowing the lawn if you move the run every day or so. If you are unable to get fresh grass, it is possible to get bales of dried grass; this differs from hay in the way it is dried. It does contain some vitamin C, although probably not as much as the best of fresh grass. Most cavies seem to enjoy the dried grass and eat up every scrap.

7. WILD FOOD

There are many plants that you can pick from the wild and feed your cavies, but, again, please do not pick from areas treated with herbicides or other sprays. And beware of poisonous plants. The best maxim is: if in doubt, leave it out of your guinea pig's diet.

POISONOUS PLANTS
- Bindweed
- Box
- Buttercups (if fed in excess – a few don't seem to matter)
- Celandine
- Deadly nightshade
- Docks (except for the very young leaves, which seem to be acceptable)

CASE HISTORY

Guinea pig Paddy went completely lame from the middle of his body down his back legs. He also lost both front teeth. It turned out that he had scurvy. None of his cagemates had the same problem, so obviously he was not absorbing enough vitamin C. With treatment he recovered, but it was really worrying. A suggested food supplement is vitamin C tablets. Guinea pigs are choosy about whether they will accept them, but it is worth persevering – some days they take them, some days they don't.

- Dog's mercury
- Elder
- Foxgloves
- Hemlock
- Honeysuckle
- Horse chestnut
- Horsetails
- Laburnum
- Laurel
- Lily of the valley
- Lords and ladies
- Monkshood
- Poppies
- Privet
- Ragwort
- Raw potato/potato leaves
- Rhubarb/rhubarb leaves
- Scarlet pimpernel
- Sorrel
- Spurge
- Wood anemone
- Yew.

ENJOYABLE PLANTS
- Clover
- Dandelions (in small amounts as they are a diuretic)
- Grass
- Groundsel

- Nettle tips and also the tips of brambles (blackberry stems).
- Plantains(both the narrow-leaved and broad-leaved type)
- Shepherd's purse
- Trefoils
- Vetches
- Young dock leaves.

> **OWNER'S TIP**
>
> *Watch your guinea pigs have fun with a scooped-out melon (you can eat most of the flesh) – but do not use a watermelon.*

8. A BALANCED DIET

The following charts show the total amount of calcium and phosphorus in one-cup portions (5 fluid ounces/ 200 ml) of selected foods. Look not only at the total milligram (mg) amount of calcium, but also the calcium:phosphorus ratio. This ratio should be close to 1:0.5 for the best calcium absorption (which is what you don't want if you are trying to prevent bladder stones). The higher the phosphorus amount compared to the calcium, the poorer the absorption of calcium is in the body (which is what you do want for a low-calcium diet). This list was originally created with birds in mind, which is why there are things such as okra and mushrooms on it. There is not much on the low-calcium list that would regularly be used to feed pigs except broccoli florets.

GOOD CALCIUM SOURCES

1 Cup Portion	Calcium	Phosphorus	Ca: Phos Ratio
Turnip greens	694 mg.	98 mg.	1: 0.14
Cabbage (outer green leaves)	429 mg.	72 mg.	1: 0.17
Chinese cabbage	400 mg.	72 mg.	1: 0.20
Broccoli leaves	349 mg.	89 mg.	1: 0.26
Watermelon	33 mg.	9 mg.	1: 0.27
Mustard greens	582 mg.	168 mg.	1: 0.29
Kohlrabi	390 mg.	120 mg.	1: 0.30
Watercress	53 mg.	15 mg.	1: 0.30
Chard	300 mg.	100 mg.	1: 0.33
Collards (cooked)	14 mg.	150 mg.	1: 0.40
Kale	390 mg.	134 mg.	1: 0.40
Dandelion greens	168 mg.	70 mg.	1: 0.40
Endive	104 mg.	39 mg.	1: 0.40
Broccoli stems	111 mg.	47 mg.	1: 0.40
Beet greens	188 mg.	80 mg.	1: 0.40

1 Cup Portion	Calcium	Phosphorus	Ca: Phos Ratio
Orange or tangerine	48 mg.	18 mg.	1: 0.40
Dark green-leaf lettuce	25 mg.	14 mg.	1: 0.56
Spinach	156 mg.	92 mg.	1: 0.60
Parsley	46 mg.	30 mg.	1: 0.65
Yellow wax beans	63 mg.	46 mg.	1: 0.70
Celery	44 mg.	32 mg.	1: 0.70

MODERATE CALCIUM SOURCES

1 Cup Portion	Calcium	Phosphorus	Ca: Phos Ratio
Cabbage (inner white leaves)	46 mg.	34 mg.	1: 0.74
Rutabaga/swede	99 mg.	75 mg.	1: 0.75
Blueberries	33 mg.	26 mg.	1: 0.80
Strawberries	68 mg.	56 mg.	1: 0.80
Summer squash	36 mg.	30 mg.	1: 0.80
Turnips	112 mg.	94 mg.	1: 0.84
Okra	144 mg.	124 mg.	1: 0.86
Carrots	90 mg.	82 mg.	1: 0.90
Cantaloupe	64 mg.	60 mg.	1: 0.90
Raspberries	82 mg.	76 mg.	1: 0.93
Green beans	55 mg.	50 mg.	1: 1.00
Blackberries	43 mg.	43 mg.	1: 1.00
Yams	44 mg.	50 mg.	1: 1.00
Guavas	15 mg.	16 mg.	1: 1.00
Apples	10 mg.	10 mg.	1: 1.00
Pears	15 mg.	18 mg.	1: 1.20

POOR CALCIUM SOURCES

1 Cup Portion	Calcium	Phosphorus	Ca: Phos Ratio
Parsnips	120 mg.	152 mg.	1: 1.30
Radish	21 mg.	29 mg.	1: 1.40
Apricots	15 mg.	21 mg.	1: 1.40
Plums	20 mg.	27 mg.	1: 1.40
Beets	56 mg.	84 mg.	1: 1.50
Cherries	19 mg.	35 mg.	1: 1.58
Cauliflower	28 mg.	46 mg.	1: 1.60
Broccoli flowers	85 mg.	140 mg.	1: 1.65
Grapes	19 mg.	35 mg.	1: 1.80
Peaches	10 mg.	19 mg.	1: 1.90
Cucumber	10 mg.	21 mg.	1: 2.10

1 Cup Portion	Calcium	Phosphorus	Ca: Phos Ratio
Pumpkin	46 mg.	100 mg.	1: 2.20
Sweet potato	19 mg.	45 mg.	1: 2.40
Lettuce (iceberg)	17 mg.	40 mg.	1: 2.40
Asparagus	28 mg.	70 mg.	1: 2.50
Tomato	11 mg.	29 mg.	1: 2.60
Eggplant/aubergine	22 mg.	62 mg.	1: 2.80
Pineapple	12 mg.	35 mg.	1: 2.90
Bananas	7 mg.	22 mg.	1: 3.10
Peas	56 mg.	254 mg.	1: 4.50
Brussels sprouts	36 mg.	161 mg.	1: 4.48
Mushrooms	19 mg.	131 mg.	1: 6.90
Corn/maize (fresh)	16 mg.	206 mg.	1: 12.90

CHAPTER 6

GUINEA PIG CARE

1. Daily care
2. Weekly care
3. Routine care
4. Emergencies
5. Health checks
6. Problem behaviour

Cavies are fairly easy to keep well and healthy, but they must have regular care. This is not very time-consuming, but it is essential for their physical and their mental wellbeing.

1. DAILY CARE

WATER

The water in the bottle should be changed regularly, as it quickly becomes unpleasant, especially in warm weather. Not all guinea pigs drink water. If they have sufficient green food and roots, they get their moisture from these.

FOOD BOWLS

If a cavy doesn't finish its food every day, it is being overfed and should have its food amounts reduced. The bowl should be washed regularly.

Any uneaten moist fresh food should be removed daily before feeding more, as it is likely to become rotten and will cause stomach upsets and attract flies.

43

BEDDING
Remember to make sure that your cavies have warm, dry bedding, especially at night. If the bedding is wet, clean out the hutch and refresh the hay. They will need much more in the winter, especially if they are housed outside, than they will in the summerr. For guinea pigs that are always housed outside, always put extra thick layers of newspaper on the hutch floor in winter. It helps to keep them warm. Check that any bedding left in the cage is dry, and top up every day.

GROOMING
All long-haired varieties, both boars and sows, must have their coats cut short before going into the breeding pen, otherwise the coats will become very matted, causing the cavies to develop sores.

Guinea pigs do not necessarily need to have any special daily grooming requirements unless they are being kept as show animals. However, most guinea pigs are happy to be brushed while being cuddled, and it is definitely advisable to regularly brush and comb a long-haired cavy to prevent its coat from becoming tangled with hay and straw.

HEALTH CHECK
Get used to assessing your pet's health. Does it look bright and active? Or is it listless with its head-down in a corner? Are its eyes clear and healthy, not dull and almost closed? If you see any change, take special notice and possibly get someone more experienced to check it out. If you think it looks ill, take it to a vet as soon as possible, as cavies are very good at hiding the fact that they are ill until the last minute. Also, they are not the easiest of animals to treat, as they seem to give up quite easily and are allergic to some common antibiotics and other medication. Luckily, they are usually healthy and rarely give problems.

2. WEEKLY CARE
On a weekly basis, cavies are still easy to care for. The cage must be cleaned out thoroughly once a week.

CAGE CARE
First, remove the cavy to a suitable box while its cage is out of bounds, and take out the food dish and water bottle. Then, using a dustpan, or something similar, scoop the rest of the contents into a bag for disposal later. If there are some stubborn patches, which have hardened, a wallpaper scraper or some other flat metal tool is useful.

44

When you have removed the soiled bedding and shavings, clean the cage by spraying it with a disinfectant suitable for use with animals. These are readily available from pet stores and supermarkets. Make sure you use the one that suits your animals, and you. The modern ones have a pleasant smell. If newspaper is used in hutches, it makes cleaning out much easier. Just roll it up – the soiled hay etc. will be rolled inside it. Then brush out the hutch and spray if needed.

When you spray, make sure you thoroughly wet the corners and the joins between the floor and sides, to kill off any unwanted pests. Also, sweep out any cobwebs in the winter because they hold the damp. If possible, wait for the disinfectant to dry and then replace the shavings with clean ones and put in some fresh bedding.

BOWLS AND WATER
Wash the food bowl just as you would a normal dish in hot water and dry before refilling it with food. The water bottle should be emptied and washed using a bottle-brush and it is a good idea to sterilise it occasionally using the solution available for babies' bottles. This reduces the growth of algae in the bottle, which makes the water very 'brackish' and unpalatable.

HEALTH
When returning the cavy to its cage, take the time to check it over. Observe its weight while you are holding it. Does it feel of similar weight to last week, or, hopefully, at least in the early days, is it putting some weight on? Is it fit, active and looking bright and happy? Is it dry and reasonably clean underneath? Are there any scabs or lumps, or are its nails in need of clipping? It is much better to try to deal with these points regularly than to have a major unnecessary problem later.

WASTE DISPOSAL
Disposal of the soiled bedding from the cage is not often a problem. If you have a garden and composter, the material can be added to the heap, where it will rot down with the other vegetative waste. The droppings will boost the fertiliser content of the finished compost. If neither you, nor anyone else you know, is able to use it in this way, you can bag it up securely and dispose of it with your household waste.

When you have several hutches to clean out, you will probably find you will need to transport the waste yourself to your nearest civic amenity rubbish tip. In many tips, providing you do not put the plastic bags in the skip, the rubbish can be composted as green-waste.

3. ROUTINE CARE
BRUSHING AND GROOMING
When handling your pet cavy, it is nice to groom it. By running a slightly damp hand (just moistened by breathing on the palm) over the coat, you will find that a considerable number of hairs can be removed. These are the coarse guard hairs and you will find that, afterwards, the coat will feel much smoother and will have a nice sheen. A piece of velvet or silk material will also impart a lovely gloss to the coat. You can also use a bristle brush to groom the cavy. The brush needs to have a fairly stiff bristle so that it can go through the hair and clean the coat properly.

Always work in the direction that the hair naturally lies, to avoid making the cavy feel uncomfortable. Most cavies have a coat that lies smooth from head to rump but some are different, and we will talk about those when we look at specific breeds.

Nail clipping
Cavies' nails grow in a similar fashion to our own. In the wild, just running on hard ground and scratching for their food would wear the nails down. As our cavies spend most of their time in a cage with very little rough surface to run on, the nails will grow quite long. Therefore they will, at some time, need trimming. Just how often will depend on the individual. It is very unusual to need to cut the toenails of a young cavy. Under five months old, all that may be necessary is to take the very pointed tip off the nail to prevent your cavies from scratching you as much when you are handling them! In fact, you will often only have to trim the hind feet of a cavy under one year old. Many people are scared of cutting the nails; however, when you have done it once or twice, it will become quite easy.

A cavy has four toes on each of its front paws and three on its back paws. The back ones are usually the ones that grow fastest. You will need a pair of nail-clippers; those designed for humans are easiest, I find. Hold the cavy on its back on your arm, and, if you look at the nail, you will be able to see where the blood vessel runs down the nail. On a light-coloured cavy, you will actually be able to see the vein but, on a dark nail, you will probably only see a slight line across the nail.

Hold the cavy's foot in your hand, and use your thumb and forefinger to hold the individual toe still. Using the clippers, just take a millimetre or so off the tip and then move on to the next nail. If done as often as you feel necessary, there will only be a small amount to trim. Regular trimming usually ensures that the nails do not become twisted and hard, although it must be said that older cavies' nails can become hard. Even then, the nail-clippers designed for toenails seem to be strong enough to handle the job.

BATHING
Cavies do not need to have daily or even weekly baths, but it can be beneficial to give them an occasional one. So why bath them? It may be that you feel their colours are looking a bit dingy, or they have become stained, or the coat has become greasy. Cavies can also become afflicted by a parasite mite that lives on the hair. These mites can be very persistent and, although they do not seem to harm the animal, it is a good idea to try to get rid of them.

It is usually best to choose a warm day if you can and, if you have more than one animal to bath, I would suggest that you bath them the same day. This is for several reasons. When you bath your cavies, you will remove some of their individual scent. If you only bathed one cavy, there is a possibility that the other animals would not recognise its smell, and may start to fight.

Also, if one is clean and the other snuggles up to it when dirty, you will be back to square one, having two dirty cavies again.

The choice of shampoo is very wide: you can use any shampoo that you would use yourself or you can use shampoos manufactured for puppies and other small animals, and these are even produced in various colours. Shampoos designed for ridding dogs of fleas can also be tried, as can herbal shampoos for the elimination of lice. You can also use shampoos that are used on human hair to clear head lice (available from chemists). The only cavies that are bathed on a very regular basis are those who are shown.

You will need to collect some items to use. Bowls of warm water, towels and shampoo are essential, and many people find a hairdryer is also useful. I find that it is easiest to use a fairly deep sink and a deep bowl, as the cavies seem to be more settled in deeper water than in a very shallow bath. Thoroughly wet the cavy all over by lowering him into the water, supporting his head with your hand so that he does not drown.

Then lift him out on to the side and work the shampoo into the coat; remember the tummy, around the legs and under his chin. Avoid getting the shampoo into the eyes – it will sting just as it does in your own. Wash inside the ears with shampoo, as mites can live in the ear wax. When you have worked up a good lather, rinse the cavy and, if you wish, add a little more shampoo and do it again. Rinse the cavy thoroughly in at least two fresh amounts of water, then lift it out of the water and wrap it in a towel. I find it easiest to have the towel ready folded in half down its length, and roll the towel round and round the animal leaving just its head poking out. I then leave the cavies to dry off for several minutes and then, using a dry towel to sit them on, I start to comb the cavy and use the hairdryer to get it completely dry.

I find that if I gently brush the hair in the opposite direction from the way it naturally grows and let the warm air blow through, I can get the cavy dried fairly quickly. Do keep the hairdryer moving all the time and do not have it on a high temperature. Avoid letting the air hurt the cavies' ears, as they do not have hair on them and could easily get burnt. Finish by giving a gentle brush in the direction the hair naturally grows. It can be a useful time to trim the cavies' nails after they have had a good soak, as the nails become softer in the water.

On a warm day, the cavy can be returned to the hutch as soon as it is dry. However, if it is wet or chilly outside, it is better to allow it to stay indoors in a box for a few hours, or even overnight, so that it doesn't get a chill. You will obviously want to return the cavy to a clean cage, so take the opportunity to give it an extra-thorough clean.

4. EMERGENCIES

Contact a vet immediately if your guinea pig:
- Shows signs of bleeding.
- Makes any kind of noise when it breathes.
- Seems to be in pain.
- Cannot or will not eat.
- Cannot or will not drink.

5. HEALTH CHECKS

Health care and diseases are covered in detail in Section II, but there are a number of conditions that the responsible owner should be aware of.

BLADDER STONES

This is a condition to which guinea pigs are prone. Pigs are used to digesting plants in the wild, which contain calcium in the form of calcium oxalate. However, alfalfa and dried food contain calcium in the form of calcium carbonate. This is absorbed much more readily and, as a result, a lot more calcium is precipitated out in the urine and can form grit and stones. One owner who had problems with her guinea pigs was advised to minimise the high-calcium foods in their diet,

48

THE PET GUINEA PIG

A guinea pig makes a wonderful addition to the family – but you must bear in mind that you are responsible for all his needs.

The correct way to hold a guinea pig.

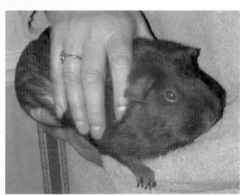

If you are tactful with handling, a guinea pig will become increasingly trusting. Let the guinea pig become familiar with your voice, and talk to him often. Cavies rely on sound, as they have poor eyesight.

49

HOUSING

An outdoor hutch should have long legs, to protect against foxes.

An outside run will be much appreciated during the summer – but a shaded area must be provided.

The run must be on even ground, so the guinea pig cannot escape underneath.

50

FEEDING

The basic ingredients of a guinea pig's diet: dry food, hay and water. Green food should also be fed daily.

Green vegetables provide a valuable source of Vitamin C.

Dry food should not be given at the same time as green food, roots and hay.

51

FEEDING

Although carrots are a firm favourite (left), a variety of fresh fruit and vegetables should be given (below).

FEEDING

Guinea pigs must have access to copious amounts of hay, as they eat large quantities of it.

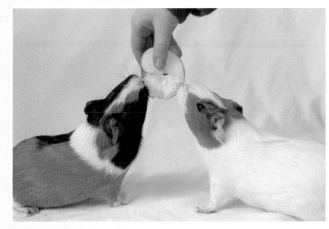

Always cut up apples so the guinea pigs have an edge to gnaw on.

Once tamed, guinea pigs enjoy being hand fed.

BREEDING

Do not breed from guinea pigs until they are over five months old. They are not full grown until they are 14 months old.

During courtship, the male (boar) does a mating dance, wagging his rear end and doing little hops.

Pregnant sows should not be handled, as the unborn piglets could be harmed.

BREEDING

Litter sizes range from one to five piglets – and sometimes there can be as many as seven.

Because of the long gestation, piglets are born very well developed. These four-day-old piglets weighed around 85 g (3 oz) at birth.

A litter of four, pictured at ten days. The piglets are born with a full coat, their eyes are open, and their teeth are already cut.

BREEDING

Three days old: These piglets are already fully mobile and independent.

The piglets are able to tackle solid food within a day of being born. Green food must be given daily, together with dry food and hay.

A sow with piglets aged two weeks. At this age, they need three meals a day.

56

which meant no kale, collard, mustard or dandelion greens, broccoli stalks or alfalfa. Instead, the guinea pigs had timothy hay, timothy-based kibble, apples, carrots, parsley, romaine, broccoli florets, and the occasional melon treat instead of apple, and grass when in season (see *Urolithasis*, page 119).

UTERINE PROBLEMS

Guinea pigs can get infected cysts, uterine infections and cancer. Unless you intend to breed your female, some vets advise getting her spayed, which can prevent problems in later life.

CALLUSES

Because of the wear and tear on guinea pigs' feet from walking around and jumping, occasionally a callus will appear. It looks and feels like a tiny hard knot on or around the pad. If it is not removed, it will eventually get bigger and bigger until it develops into 'bumble foot', which is a very different matter.

CASE HISTORY

When taking Crumpet out of his cage to hold him, his owner noticed he was breathing very strangely and wheezing, so promptly called the vet and got in the car. The vet thought that Crumpet had allergies and prescribed an antihistamine to give him orally, with a syringe, for the following 15 days. This made sense, since Crumpet had a tendency to sneeze during the same times as the owner's allergies were bad, and he didn't have any symptoms of infection.

The problem seemed to be pollen and dust. Although Crumpet is an indoor-only pig, it is obvious why he could still have trouble. He lives in a area with a high pollen count, although his owner, also suffering from hay fever, keeps the apartment as allergen-free as possible. The intense heat did not help either.

Luckily, the weather cooled down and that, combined with the antihistamine, helped Crumpet. His breathing got much better. He did not like the syringe, but he learned to co-operate. The treatment only lasted 15 days because it was like a human getting allergy shots. After a certain period of time, the person develops a higher tolerance for the allergen and only needs medication as a booster during intense allergy seasons.

It is important to check the feet for any distortion or hard patches. A weekly rub with an appropriate cream will prevent problems, and will also get rid of any hard skin. Some guinea pigs love having their feet massaged; with others there might be a bit of difficulty, but persevere. Another tip is to use udder cream on the feet.

> **Top tip:** *For a guinea pig with foot trouble, use a synthetic, fleecy veterinary bedding, which is nice and soft. For a pig with dry skin on its feet, keep them clean and apply vitamin E oil daily.*

BUMBLE FOOT

This starts off with a sore on the foot, which becomes crusted over. Meanwhile, an infection starts to grow and accumulates pus inside the wound. Walking will be painful and will irritate it. It can also cause the wound to split wide open and spread infection inside the cage to other sores, such as scratches or bites. The worst thing that can happen is that the whole foot swells up and becomes too painful to walk on. If this splits open, the guinea pig could bleed to death. Obviously, the guinea pig should be taken to the vet long before the callus gets to such an advanced stage.

TEETH

Cavies can have problems with their teeth, but it is possible to have them filed. They do not necessarily need to have an anaesthetic to have

CASE HISTORY

Two females were diagnosed with ovarian cysts at four and five years of age. One had symmetrical areas of hair loss on the sides of her abdomen and the other had random hair loss all over her belly. This was not responsive to treatment for mites and the pig seemed quite uncomfortable when being picked up. Neither pig seemed itchy. The cysts were diagnosed by using ultrasound and were treated by spaying both pigs. They did fine through the surgery and did very well post-op with pain-management medicine. There is also a growth hormone, which is administered through injection, that can be used to try to manage the cysts without surgery, but it does not always work and has to be repeated regularly. Some reports state that the incidence of ovarian cysts can be up to 80 per cent in older unspayed females.

this done. Some vets have an instrument that will keep the pig's mouth open while the teeth are filed.

SCENT GLANDS

Cavies have a scent gland situated on the rump, just above the anus, approximately where you would imagine their tail should be. It is also known as the grease gland. It exudes a sticky substance that, when living in the wild, would be scraped on to the ground or on to plants to mark their territory. The gland gets much stickier in males than females. If, as is often the case, the guinea pig's rump becomes dirty and greasy, this can be cleaned off using washing-up liquid or the gel used to remove oil and grease from hands. Just rub it gently into the area, working it into the hair and rinsing it off when the area is clean. You may find that this leaves a small bald patch, but the hair will grow back again although, due to the gland, some males are inclined to have a small clear area here. On long-haired breeds, if the hair becomes very sticky, it gets matted and tangled up with bits of hay and shavings. If these are left, the hair will eventually need to be cut to remove them. To avoid this, it is a good idea to brush and clean the scent gland area regularly if you wish to keep the coat long.

SEBACEOUS CYSTS

Humans have these as well as guinea pigs. It is where an oil gland becomes blocked and the oil builds up into a waxy substance called sebum. The vet will be able to take care of it. A sebaceous cyst can be non-active, which means that, after it is opened up, it begins to dry up and heal with treatment. However, if it gets infected, or continues to produce liquid matter, it probably needs to be excised.

RED URINE

This has to be taken seriously because it could be indicative of some serious medical problem, if the colour is caused by blood. However, it could also be that your guinea pig has eaten too much red beetroot! How to tell the difference: blood in the urine is usually confined to a bright red in the middle and clear urine away from that area; 'beet pee' is a uniform dark colour (see page 114]).

STOMACH IMPACTION

This is, to put it simply, when the gut gets sluggish or stops working. The guinea pig emits few or no faeces and is in pain. There used to be a theory that giving the animal mineral oil would help, but this has largely been disproved. There is also disapproval of the use of antibiotics to cure the condition. The best thing to do is to seek the advice of a vet immediately.

PARASITES
Guinea pigs can pick up mites and lice. There are preparations that can treat both infestations. Sometimes mites cause bald patches to appear. If your guinea pig seems to be scratching its rear end with its water bottle, for example, or rubbing up against any surface, even a paper bag, look for lice. Guinea pigs can also be susceptible to ringworm, for which dip baths are the cure.

INJURIES
Sometimes a guinea pig can get its foot caught in an obstruction, which is why most pet owners dislike the cage flooring to be made of wire. Such injuries happen particularly when the animal is in jumping mood. Usually the leg then breaks.

Some vets will operate and some guinea pigs will survive. It has even been known for a guinea pig to have a leg amputated after such an injury and live to see four more years. However, since guinea pigs are delicate as far as anaesthetics and medication are concerned, there are risks involved.

HOT WEATHER TIPS
Remember to keep an eye on guinea pigs in hot weather. If you are due for a very hot day, try some of these ideas.
• Fill a clean plastic soda bottle two-thirds full of water and freeze. On a hot day, place it against a wall in the guinea pig's area so your pet can lie near or against it.
• Be sure the cavy's area is not in direct sun and has good air flow.
• Food should not be fed directly from the fridge. Leave it to get to room temperature.
• In very hot weather try not to disturb the guinea pigs too much. Repeatedly rousing them and picking them up distresses them even more.

6. PROBLEM BEHAVIOUR
Some guinea pigs seem obsessed with chewing the bars of their cages. They seem to do this when they want to be fed, or when they want attention and they want it NOW. Give them some hay and they should be satisfied.

BITING
Most pets will mouth their owners. Think of a small puppy, who wants to get its mouth around everything within range. With guinea pigs, the problem is a little different, as their teeth are so strong. If bitten when feeding a guinea pig, it's because it cannot see your fingers – the pig assumes you are food!

TIMIDITY
Here are some tips that can help the shy guinea pig.
• Make sure that all hiding places are eliminated.
• Talk to your guinea pig so that it gets used to the tone of your voice.
• When the pig is used to you, then you can start picking it up.
• Introduce the guinea pig to other people.
• Once a guinea pig really knows you, it will trust you to pick it up. If you hold it properly, it will soon become less shy.

CASE HISTORY

Trudy was a young guinea pig brought into a loving home, but she was truly terrified of being touched. The owner tried to pick her up gently, to give her a health check, but she evaded this. The owner's boyfriend, who was the one who had bought Trudy as a special gift, finally quietly caught her. But she would not be held. She would not take food from their hands, but she would nibble cereals when she thought they were not looking. The answer is, don't rush it with a new guinea pig – some will become friendly more readily than others. Just persevere. Some humans are touchy-feely, some are not. Give guinea pigs the same latitude.

CHAPTER 7

ANATOMY AND PHYSIOLOGY

1. Skeleton
2. Teeth
3. Digestive system
4. Senses
5. Liver and kidneys
6. Respiratory system
7. Heart
8. Reproduction

The guinea pig is a relatively large rodent with a short neck, a cobby body, short legs and no signs of an exterior tail. The shape of the ears varies; they can be small and upright in many cross-bred pigs, and large, rose-petal-shaped and drooping in pure-bred specimens. The ears have only sparse or non-existent coat, and behind each ear there is a bald area.

The coat is short, smooth and about 2 cm (just under 1 inch) long. There are, however, breeds with other coat types. Several different colours and markings are recognised. A single pig may have up to three different colours.

On the guinea pig's rear there is a grease gland, which is well developed in the boar. Two nipples are placed in the groin of both sexes. There are four toes on each front leg and three on each hind leg. Guinea pigs walk on their heels, just like humans and other rodents. The average adult weighs 900-1200 g (approximately 2-2.6 lbs), with boars tending to be a bit larger than sows.

Body temperature in a healthy guinea pig varies between 36.5 and 39.5 degrees Celsius (96 and 103 degrees Fahrenheit). Temperature is taken by putting a thermometer in the rectum, which can be a little difficult to find. A lower temperature is a very serious sign, indicating that the pig is too weak to maintain body temperature, but it may also simply reflect the fact that the thermometer is not placed properly in the rectum. High temperatures are caused by infections, pain and certain tumours.

PHYSIOLOGICAL DATA OF GUINEA PIGS

Adult weight: 900-120 g (2-2.6lb.)
Average life span: 4-6 years
Tooth formula: 1 incisor, 1 premolar and 3 molars in each quadrant
Body temperature: 36.5-39.5 degrees Celsius (96-103F)
Pulse: 230-380/minute
Respiration: 42-104/minute

1. SKELETON

Guinea pigs have 258 bones in total. However, 22 of them are fused and form the skull and face. Together with the two mandibular bones, they make up the head. The smallest bones in the body are the three middle ear bones: malleus, incus and stapes.

The spinal column consists of 34 vertebrae: 7 cervical, 13 thoracic, 6 lumbar, 1 sacral and 7 coccygeal (tail) vertebrae. There are 26 ribs, 13 on each side. Every rib is attached to one of the thoracic vertebrae. Underneath, the front ribs are fixed to the sternal bones (of which there are 5) forming the rib cage, while the last ribs have no attachment underneath and are called 'false ribs'.

Each front leg consists of 43 bones. The scapula is the shoulder blade; next is the humerus, which is the bone of the upper arm. The lower arm has two bones, the ulna and the radius. Then follow the 10 carpal bones, 4 metatarsals and finally 12 digit bones, 3 for each of the 4 toes. Finally, there are a number of sesamoid bones, which are formed by the tendons to protect them when they pass certain joints.

The pelvis consists of 3 bones: ileum, ischium and pubis. The pubic bones are fused underneath in the so-called symphysis, but, when a sow is due for birth, the symphyses loosen and a fissure up to two fingers wide separates the pubic bones. This makes the sow able to deliver her large babies.

Each hind leg has 36 bones. The femur is connected to the pelvis in the hip joint. The stifle joint is next, with the patella, tibia and fibula.

Skeleton of a Guinea Pig

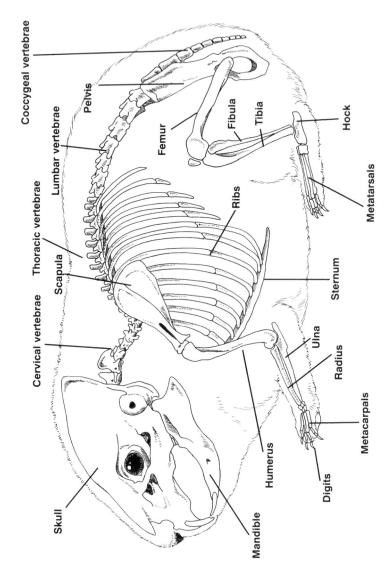

Then follows the hock, with calcaneus, thallus and 7 tarsal bones, 3 metatarsal and 3 digit bones in each toe, 9 in all. Again, there are a number of sesamoid bones.

Finally, the guinea pig has a penis bone, which is approximately 1 cm long (0.4 inches). It is not unusual for animals to have a penis bone. It is seen, for example, in whales, bulls, dogs and tomcats.

2. TEETH

Babies are born with a full set of permanent teeth. However, there is evidence that they develop a set of deciduous teeth first, which are lost in utero. The guinea pig has 20 teeth in all, 5 in each quadrant of the mouth.

The four incisors (front teeth) are situated just behind the lips. They are covered by enamel on the front surface only. As the softer dentine behind the enamel layer is worn down more quickly, a chisel shape occurs making incisors very sharp and specially designed for gnawing. Front teeth are white, which is unusual, as most rodents have an orange-brown enamel due to deposits of iron compounds.

There are no canine (corner) teeth. Instead, there is a large gap called the diastema. The lips form panniculi, or cheek pads, which protrude into the diastema, making it impossible to look inside the oral cavity without special instruments and, in most cases, full anaesthesia.

Teeth: Side view

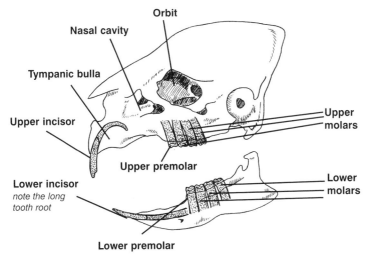

65

Teeth: Front view

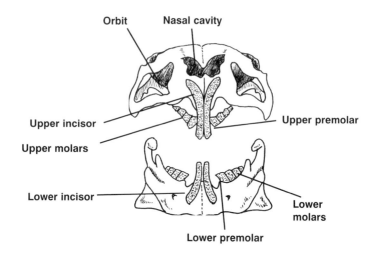

Deep inside the oral cavity, the cheek teeth are situated, with one premolar and three molars in each side. These are placed at an angle of approximately 30 degrees. The mandibular (lower) teeth are wider apart than the maxillary (upper) teeth. The cheek teeth chew the food with approximately 200 side-to-side movements per minute.

The natural food of guinea pigs is grass, straw and herbage growing in the grass. This is coarse, fibre rich, low in energy and highly abrasive, resulting in considerable tooth wear. Therefore, guinea pig teeth are open-rooted and grow continuously throughout life. The tooth crowns are long, and teeth protrude deep into the jaws.

Guinea pigs have several muscles of mastication. The masseter muscle, however, is the most important. The mandible is able to move backwards and forwards depending on which teeth the guinea pig is using. At resting position, the lower incisor teeth are situated just behind the upper. When gnawing, the mandible is moved forwards, placing the lower incisors right beneath the upper. For chewing, the mandible moves backwards, bringing upper and lower cheek teeth into place.

The guinea pig's tongue is long and narrow, and most of it is fixed to the floor of the oral cavity. Only the tip of the tongue is able to move freely. When chewing, food is mixed with saliva and swallowed. The food reaches the stomach through the oesophagus (the gullet).

66

3. DIGESTIVE SYSTEM

The stomach is a thin-walled, fluid-filled sac. A fold in the mucous membrane of the stomach covers the entrance from the oesophagus, making reflux from stomach to oesophagus impossible. This means that the guinea pig is unable to vomit.

In the stomach, gastric juices containing acid and enzymes are produced in order to break down food proteins into amino acids, which will be absorbed in the small intestines. When entering the small intestines, the environment becomes alkaline due to secretions from the

Digestive system

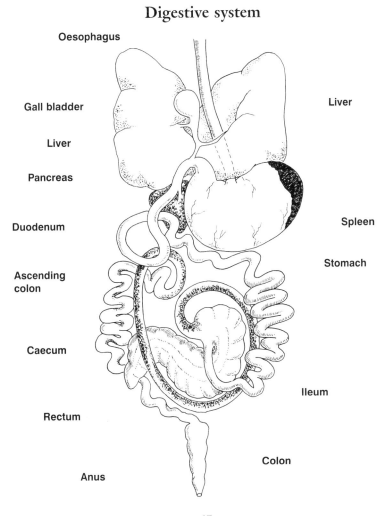

Oesophagus

Gall bladder

Liver

Pancreas

Duodenum

Ascending colon

Caecum

Rectum

Anus

Liver

Spleen

Stomach

Ileum

Colon

pancreas. Pancreatic enzymes break down starch into sugars and fat into triglycerides and fatty acids, aided by gall produced by the liver. Everything is absorbed by the small intestines. After absorption of proteins, starch and fat, fibres are left undigested until they enter the hind gut, which consists of the colon and caecum.

The caecum, and the first section of colon, act as large fermentation chambers. In fact they occupy 50-75 per cent of the space in the abdominal cavity. In the hind gut, fibres are sorted through complicated gut movements into large, indigestible fibres, which are passed on through the colon, and the small digestible fibres, which are fermented.

In the hind gut, the environments are stable, with a constant temperature, oxygen tension and pH that favours the growth of bacteria, which are able to use the cellulose of the small fibres to produce energy for further bacterial growth. If the delicate balance in the hind gut is disturbed, harmful bacteria will multiply at the expense of the normal gut flora, which causes intestinal disease. This may be seen after rapid food changes and the use of inappropriate antibiotics.

FAECES

Guinea pigs produce two different types of stools. The first kind is the well-known dry, firm, brown and elongated droppings. These consist of indigestible fibres with a low water content, as residual water is absorbed in the colon. The second kind is the caecotrophes. These are the result of bacterial fermentation in the hind gut. They are softer, with a higher water content compared to normal stools. They are also rich in protein and vitamins, in particular vitamin K and different B-vitamins. Caecotrophes are seldom seen, as the guinea pig eats them directly from the anus. However, in old boars, impaction of the rectum with caecotrophes may be seen.

Guinea pigs produce up to 150 caecotrophes every day. The coarser and more fibre-rich the food, the more important the caecotrophes become for the wellbeing of the guinea pig. On the contrary, if food is a high-calorie diet with a high protein content, caecotrophes become a less important part of nutrition.

FOOD TRANSIT TIME

Food transit time is 24 hours on average, but varies from a few hours to several days. Fibres are very important, not only for nutrition but also for producing the bulk material, which stimulates gut motility and drives the food through the intestines. If the intake of fibres is insufficient, due to feeding high-calorie diets, or if tooth problems prevent the guinea pig from eating coarse food items, gut motility is decreased and harmful micro-organisms may produce overgrowth, causing digestive disturbances.

4. SENSES

SIGHT

The eyes are large and placed on each side of the head. The field of vision is extensive, making the guinea pig able to detect efficiently predators coming from above or from any angle on the ground. But it is unable to see anything straight in front of its nose. Sight is not particularly good, but guinea pigs are able to see moving objects and it is believed that they can see colours as well.

The eye is covered by a translucent and protective membrane, called the cornea. The surface of the cornea is kept moist by secretions (tears) from the lachrymal glands. One of these glands produces tears that have a milky white appearance and are commonly seen in the corners of the eye during grooming. This should not be mistaken for conjunctivitis.

Behind the cornea, the iris can be seen. This is dark brown in most pigs, but pink-eyed variants are also quite common. The pupil is the central round opening in the iris. Light passes through the cornea and pupil to the lens. It is then refracted and projected on to the retina in the back wall of the eye, where light-sensitive cells are situated. These cells give information through the optic nerve into the brain where all information is assembled to form what is perceived as a picture.

SOUND

The guinea pig's sense of hearing is very good, and they can hear frequencies inaudible to the human ear. The ear canal is short and narrow and, at the far end, the ear drum acts as a blind end. Sound waves pass through the outer ear and hit the ear drum, causing it to vibrate. These vibrations are transmitted through the middle ear via the ear bones – the malleus, incus and stapes – into the inner ear. There, the vibrations are transformed into nerve impulses, which are transmitted through the auditory nerve into the brain, where sound perception is situated.

SMELL

The olfactory sense is well developed in the guinea pig. A smell is actually composed of small airborne molecules. When these are inhaled, they are transported through the nasal cavity to the far end, where they are registered by sensitive cells in the mucous membrane. From here there is only a short journey via the olfactory nerve into the olfactory centre of the brain.

TASTE
Taste is closely linked to the sense of smell, but it is unknown which tastes are well perceived in the guinea pig.

TOUCH
Touch is a very important sense in the guinea pig. The tactile hairs situated around the eyes, mouth and nostrils (the whiskers) are especially sensitive and help when the guinea pig is moving around in darkness. The senses of touch and smell are very important when choosing food items, as, due to their eye placement, guinea pigs are unable to see what they eat.

5. LIVER AND KIDNEYS

These are two vital organs. The liver, as mentioned under the digestive system, plays a role in fat and carbohydrate (starch) digestion. However, this organ has many other functions. The liver is situated in the foremost part of the abdominal cavity just behind the diaphragm, which is the division between the thoracic and abdominal cavity. Some of the other important functions are detoxification of metabolic by-products, such as ammonia from protein metabolism, which is transformed to urea and excreted by the kidneys; storage of vitamins; the production of proteins important in the blood and factors necessary for blood coagulation and the production of fat compounds.

Liver failure always leads to death. The most important cause of liver failure is pregnancy toxaemia, where large amounts of fat are deposited in the liver, causing fatty liver degeneration.

The kidneys are about 2 cm (just under 1 inch) long and situated in the abdominal cavity just beneath the spine and behind the last ribs. The main function of the kidneys is the excretion of toxic by-products from metabolism and excess amounts of salts, but hormones regulating blood pressure and the production of red blood cells (EPO) are also produced. When blood is passed through the kidneys, water, together with certain salts, are filtered out, forming the pre-urine. This is modified when passing through the kidney. Water and some salts are reabsorbed, while waste products, of which urea is the most important, are actively secreted, together with other salts.

From the kidneys, urine passes through the ureters to the urinary bladder where urine is stored. From the urinary bladder, urine passes on through the urethra. In the boar, the urethra is a long and narrow tube ending in the penis. In the sow, the urethra is shorter and wider, and runs into a tiny hole, the urinary orifice, which is placed just above the hymen. Guinea pig urine is quite concentrated, opaque and thick, often with a high content of calcium crystals. Urine pH is rather alkaline, about 8.5. The colour is yellow to light brown, occasionally stained by porphyrin, a red dye. This should not be mistaken for blood.

Kidney failure is quite common in older pigs. This means that the kidneys lose the ability to concentrate urine, the urine becomes thinner, the guinea pig urinates more and consequently drinks more also, in an attempt to compensate for excessive fluid loss through the kidneys.

6. RESPIRATORY SYSTEM

The respiratory rate is quite high – 42-104 breaths per minute. Air passes through the nostrils and the nasal cavity to the pharynx. From here it flows through the larynx, where the vocal cord is situated. This is where the widely-varied and much-loved guinea pig sounds are produced.

From the larynx, air flows through the trachea (the air pipe), which divides into the main bronchi and a number of minor bronchi, distributing air into all parts of the lung. Finally, air reaches the alveoli – extremely thin pouches (just one cell layer), which are in direct contact with the small lung capillaries (microscopic blood vessels). This close contact makes the exchange of gases possible. Oxygen from the alveoli flows into the bloodstream, while carbon dioxide flows from the capillaries to the alveoli and is exhaled.

The thoracic cavity in the guinea pig is small and narrow, and the lungs are small. This means that, although the guinea pig moves quickly when escaping from danger, it is a sprinter and not designed for long-distance exercise.

7. HEART

The heart is an ever-working muscle, which lies centrally in the thoracic cavity just above the sternal bone. Guinea pigs have a rapid heart rate of 230-380 beats per minute. From the right half of the heart, blood is pumped into the lungs, where oxygen uptake and carbon dioxide excretion take place. Oxygen in the blood is transported by a protein called haemoglobin, which is red and thus responsible for the colour of the blood. The oxygen-rich blood is now returned to the left half of the heart from where it is pumped out into the rest of the body. Sudden death due to heart failure is regarded as quite common.

Blood is distributed throughout the body through blood vessels. Arteries are thick-walled vessels through which blood is pumped from the heart. The main body artery is called the aorta and leads blood backwards to the abdominal cavity and rear end. Smaller arteries (e.g. for the kidneys, the ovaries and the uterus) stem from the aorta on its way through the abdominal cavity. The arteries branch out and finally end in the capillary system, which consists of microscopic vessels. Through the capillaries, every single cell in the body is supplied with oxygen and nourishment, and waste products are removed. On the way back to the heart, blood is transported through thinner vessels than the arteries, called veins.

Blood consists of fluid (blood plasma) and cells. Blood plasma contains several vital proteins, e.g. albumin for transporting other substances around, globulin that protects antibodies, and fibrinogen, which is essential for blood coagulation.

Blood cells are divided into erythrocytes (red blood cells), leucocytes (white blood cells) and thrombocytes. These are all produced in the bone marrow. Erythrocytes contain haemoglobin, which binds the oxygen while it is transported in the bloodstream. When oxygen is bound to haemoglobin, it has a bright red colour, while haemoglobin not binding oxygen is blue. That explains why mucous membranes in an oxygen-deficient animal turn blue. Anaemia is lack of erythrocytes.

The two most common causes for anaemia in the guinea pig are bleeding (i.e. during birth) and kidney failure (reduced production of EPO).

There are different sorts of leucocytes, but, in one way or another, they all play a part in the immune system, either by ingesting foreign material such as a virus or bacteria, by producing antibodies, or by excreting substances that have other functions in disease control, e.g. by triggering fever.

In the case of an infectious disease, large amounts of leucocytes are produced and released in the bloodstream from the bone marrow. This can be detected when a blood sample is examined under the microscope.

Thrombocytes are cell fragments formed by a particular cell in the bone marrow. Their main function is to prevent excessive bleeding. In the case of blood vessel damage, thrombocytes immediately start adhering to the wall, thus closing the hole.

8. REPRODUCTION

MALE
The penis is situated just above the anal opening and is hidden within the prepuce. On the tip of the penis there are two spikes, each about 5 mm (0.2 inches) long. Their function is unknown, but absence of one or both spikes has been associated with infertility. Inside the penis is a penis bone, about 1 cm (0.4 inches) long in the adult boar.

The testicles are positioned on each side of the anal/prepuce opening. They look very large, but more than half of their size is due to fat deposits that absorb bumps when the guinea pig moves around. The testicles have, in common with all male animals, two main functions. They produce sperm cells and the male hormone testosterone. Testosterone is responsible for male sexual behaviour.

After formation, sperm cells are stored in the adjacent structure, the epididymis, where they mature. Upon ejaculation, sperm cells are transported through the spermatic ducts. On the way, they pass the male sex glands: the seminal vesicles, the prostate gland and the bulbourethral gland. Secretions from the first two glands nourish and further mature the sperm cells. The mixture of secretions and sperm cells is called semen. After ejaculating the semen, the bulbourethral glands secrete a fluid, which coagulates, forming a plug in the vagina of the sow, preventing the semen from running out again. Occasionally, if the boar has ejaculated outside the vagina, the coagulated bulbourethral secretions can be seen as a white mass resembling hardened candle wax in the coat of the sow. Sexual maturity for boars is reached at 6-8 weeks of age, at a weight of 400-600 g (14-21 oz).

FEMALE
The ovaries are situated inside the abdomen. They produce egg cells and the hormones necessary for ovulation and the establishment and maintenance of pregnancy. In sows older than 2-3 years, cystic ovaries are very common. Instead of releasing eggs, fluid-filled blisters are formed. Such ovarian cysts are a common cause of infertility in older sows.

The eggs are released into a funnel-like structure called the

Female Reproductive System

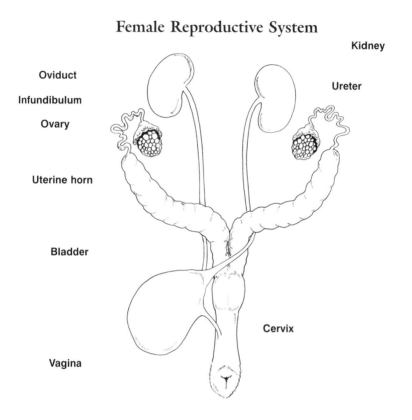

infundibulum, which leads into the oviduct where fertilisation takes place should mating have occurred.

The uterus consists of two tube-like structures, the cornua. Each cornua has its own cervix, which leads into a common vagina. The genital opening may be difficult to see, as it is covered by a thin membrane, the hymen, most of the time. Only during oestrus and parturition does the hymen open for a short period of time.

Sexual maturity for a sow occurs at 3-5 weeks of age when her weight is 300-400 g (10.5-14 oz). The sow comes into season (oestrus) every 16th day for a few hours. The hymen will break and there is free passage into the vagina, which is swollen and bluish-pink with a slimy vaginal discharge. The sow will change her behaviour as well. She will make growling sounds and, if stroked over the rear end, will lift it into a mating position. If kept with other sows, she will act like a boar, mounting her cagemates. During oestrus, the sow will release 1-6 eggs from the ovaries. This process is called ovulation.

REPRODUCTIVE DATA OF GUINEA PIGS

Sexual maturity, sow	4-6 weeks
Sexual maturity, boars	6-8 weeks
Sexual cycle, sow	6 days
Length of gestation	64-72 days
Litter size	1-6 (average 3-5)
Newborn weight	50-130 g (1.8-4.6 oz)
Weaning	Minimum 4 weeks and 300 g (10.5 oz).

MATING AND FERTILISATION

When in oestrus, most sows will allow any boar to mate them. A few, however, will not accept a boar she is unfamiliar with and will refuse.

Mating takes place several times during an oestrus period. Each mating takes only a few seconds and will sometimes be repeated after just a minute. The sperm cells will find their way through the cervix and cornua into the oviduct. The coagulating secretion from the male bulbourethral glands will form a plug in the vagina, preventing the semen from running out of the vagina. Occasionally, such a plug can be found in the cage a few days after mating. If egg cells are present in the oviducts, fertilisation will take place. Normally all ovulated egg cells are fertilised.

The fertilised egg soon begins dividing, creating an embryo of 2, 4 and 8 cells. In the beginning, all cells are identical but soon the differentiation process begins, leading to the formation of germ tissues which then develop into various organ systems. The embryo is transported by oviduct movement into the cornua, where implantation takes place. This is a process through which the embryos come into contact with, and become settled into, the uterine mucous membrane. Soon, the foetal membranes are formed and a connection between the foetus and the uterus develops, making it possible for the embryo to receive nutrition from the mother.

The embryo has now developed into a foetus, which soon takes the shape of a tiny baby guinea pig. The foetuses are located side by side in the uterine cornua like pearls on a string. While developing, the foetus is in close contact with the mother through the placenta. This is an organ that consists of a foetal side, formed by the foetus, and a maternal side, formed by the mother. In the placenta, the blood from the mother comes into close contact with the blood from the foetus, which makes it possible for nutrients and oxygen to enter the foetus while carbon dioxide and waste products leave the foetus and enter the mother. Blood vessels from the placenta enter the foetus through the umbilical cord.

Maintenance of pregnancy is a complicated process, which depends upon the interactions between sex hormones produced in the pituitary gland, the ovaries and the uterus. A gland called corpus luteum is formed at each site of ovulation. This produces progesterone, which is important in maintaining pregnancy as it prevents the pregnant sow from coming into oestrus. After approximately 30 days of pregnancy, however, progesterone production is taken over by the uterus.

MONITORING THE PREGNANCY
The first sign of pregnancy is the absence of oestrus 16 days after mating, a signal that is often overlooked by guinea pig owners. Early uterus enlargement can be felt by hand, usually at 3-5 weeks of pregnancy, but its detection depends a lot upon the skills of the person doing the investigation.

Weighing the sow once weekly will show a marked increase in weight at 4 weeks, which continues for the rest of the pregnancy. At 6.5 to 7 weeks after mating, foetal movements can be felt when holding a hand under the sow's belly.

Just before birth, the belly is grossly distended and movement is restricted. Babies may constitute up to one-third of the sow's total body weight. Foetal movements are easily seen, and foetal parts, such as the head and legs, can be felt.

Occasionally, it is even possible to hear the babies' teeth grinding. A sow is pregnant for 64 to 72 days. This is a long pregnancy compared to other rodents. The reason is that guinea pigs do not live in hollows, so babies have to be well developed and able to move around immediately after birth.

BIRTH
Between 4 and 10 days before birth, the pelvic bones begin to open. This process is essential, as guinea pig babies are very large and this movement allows them to pass through the birth canal. If the sow is having her first litter at later than one year of age, there is an increased risk that the pelvic bones will have become rigid and will be unable to widen. This will result in a prolonged birth with the risk of stillborn babies and maybe even death of the sow.

The opening of the pelvis is easily felt by placing a finger under the guinea pig a few centimetres in front of the anal opening. When the opening is as wide as 1 to 2 fingers, most sows will give birth within 48 hours.

Immediately before the sow gives birth to her first baby, the hymen will break. Some sows utter a few wails when this happens. The sow gives birth in a standing position. It takes only a few seconds and a couple of birth contractions to expel the baby. The mother turns around immediately to bite off the umbilical cord and to remove foetal membranes from the head, allowing the baby to breathe. Afterwards, the sow cleans the baby from head to rear. Within 5 to 10 minutes, the next baby arrives and the sow repeats the procedure.

Occasionally, a baby is born rear-first, which does not seem to complicate the birth though it may lead an inexperienced sow to try to remove the foetal membranes from the wrong end. If the baby is too weak to break through on its own, it may die from suffocation.

A litter can consist of 1 to 6 babies, with 3 to 4 being the most common litter size. The sow expels one placenta for each baby and, usually, she cleans herself and the surroundings so efficiently that only little blood is left in the bedding.

A few hours after giving birth, the sow comes into oestrus again. This is the so-called post-partum oestrus. If mated, sows usually become pregnant again, making them able to give birth to a litter every 9 to 10 weeks. Most fanciers avoid post-partum matings by removing the boar before the expected birth, as they consider it too stressful for the sow to rear a litter and be pregnant at the same time.

GUINEA PIG BABIES

Guinea pig babies are well developed at birth with eyes open, a full coat and permanent teeth. Birth weight varies between 50 and 130 g (1.8-4.6 oz), depending mainly on the litter size. Some studies suggest that guinea pigs have a set of deciduous teeth, which are lost in the uterus.

Babies can move around and follow their mum as soon as they are born. They start eating solid food from day one, as a supplement to their mother's milk provided from two nipples situated between the hind legs. The babies grow quickly, and weaning age is reached in 4 to 6 weeks at the minimum weight of 300 g (10.6 oz).

CHAPTER 8

A-Z OF GUINEA PIG DISEASES & HEALTH PROBLEMS

Alphabetical listing of guinea pig dieases and health problems

Although guinea pigs can suffer from a wide range of illnesses, there are four dominating diseases that make up 90 per cent or more of all cases. These are usually named 'the four killer diseases'. They should be familiar to, and, if possible, prevented by, any guinea pig breeder and fancier. The four diseases are malocclusion, vitamin C deficiency (scurvy), mange, and pregnancy toxaemia (see below). It is often difficult to detect disease at an early stage as guinea pigs are prey animals, and they tend to hide symptoms for quite a period.

ABSCESSES

The result of an infection in which pus is produced. The infected area is surrounded by an abscess capsule, which limits the infection.

An abscess may form at any site. Bite wounds penetrating the skin are very likely to develop into abscesses. Tooth abscesses are infrequently seen (see Malocclusion). Foot abscesses may be seen in older, overweight animals. The foot is swollen and sore (see Pododermatitis). A special kind of abscess is seen in younger animals and is due to an infection with streptococcal bacteria (see Cervical lymphadenitis).

No matter the cause, an abscess always develops the same way. First, there are the typical signs of inflammation. The affected area is swollen, red, warm and sore. In the beginning, the inflammation is diffuse. Later, it becomes more well defined when the abscess is formed by producing a fibrous capsule to demarcate the infection. If the abscess is situated under the skin (as in a bite abscess), the abscess grows, hair begins to fall off and the skin turns bluish. Finally, the skin bursts and the pus is released on to the skin surface.

The pus is full of bacteria and care should be taken to prevent other pigs from licking it off, as this may lead to serious infections. If taken to the surgery in time, it is better to let the veterinarian incise the abscess in a controlled way. After the pus has been removed, the capsule must be rinsed and disinfected and an antibiotic treatment may be instituted if necessary. Often, the hole is left open so that newly formed pus can drain.

ABORTION
Miscarriage in the mid or last trimester of pregnancy where the sow expels the foetus and foetal membranes.

There are many causes for abortion. Developmental defects in foetuses or foetal membranes are quite common. Although it occasionally happens that only a single foetus dies and mummifies (see Mummification) while the rest of the litter is carried to term, it is more common that the whole litter is lost. Other causes of abortion include stress, nutritional deficiencies (see Vitamin C deficiency), and concomitant diseases, e.g. mange, loud noises, or falls.

Abortion is seen in any stage of pregnancy. Abortion during the first trimester of pregnancy is often unnoticed by the owner (see Resorption). Abortion in the second trimester is often quite uncomplicated. The sow expels her dead litter quite easily, without showing signs of discomfort or illness. The first sign is bleeding from the vagina. After the miscarriage, she usually cleans up so well that a slight stain of blood around the nose or on the vent may be the only signs.

If sows abort during the last three weeks of gestation, the symptoms are often more alarming and there is a great risk of complications (see Pregnancy toxaemia, and Metritis). The sow is often depressed and anorectic, and many sows will die.

AGALACTIA
The sow produces little or no milk for her suckling babies.

Agalactia may be caused by stress, malnutrition or other diseases, e.g. toxaemia or infections. The babies become restless and aggressive and have a lean stomach. They may damage the nipples, making the sow feel uncomfortable and irritated (see Sore nipples), and the weakest babies may die. An injection with oxytocin may help bring down the milk, otherwise feeding with juicy greens may increase milk production. It may be necessary to hand rear the babies (see Orphan babies).

ANOPHTHALMIA
Babies are white and born without eyes.
See Microphthalmia.

ANOREXIA
The guinea pig does not eat.
When dealing with an anorectic guinea pig, it is important to find the cause. It is very critical if a guinea pig does not eat for a couple of days, especially if she is pregnant (see Pregnancy toxaemia), but any anorectic pig will soon deteriorate and die unless a cause is identified and treated.

There are two main reasons for anorexia – loss of ability to eat because of overgrown teeth (see Malocclusion), or loss of appetite caused by illness. In the first case, the guinea pig seems well, alert and hungry, but gives up eating after a few bites. In the latter, the pig is depressed and shows no interest in food, not even if favourites are offered. Sometimes, pigs stop eating for no obvious reason, and such pigs are difficult to deal with.

When the cause of anorexia is under treatment it is important to encourage the pig to eat treats, and hand-feeding may become necessary. If it is still not eating, force-feeding is the only option.

Commercial baby foods are just as suitable as they are for hand-feeding babies (see Orphan babies). Appetite stimulants, such as vitamin B, 0.5 – 1 cc of liquor (it is no joke, it actually works sometimes), glucocorticoid injections, etc. may help. But unfortunately, many pigs seem to give up and lose the will for living, and for such pigs there is no hope.

ANTIBIOTIC TOXICITY
An overgrowth of clostridia bacteria caused by antibiotics, which kills the normal healthy intestinal flora.
In the hind gut where microbial fermentation of dietary fibres takes

place, the environment must be within very narrow limits of pH, temperature and chemical composition, to ensure optimal conditions for the normal and healthy flora. Harmful micro-organisms are found in small numbers but are controlled by the healthy flora. Many antibiotics, e.g. penicillin, kill the normal and beneficial bacteria allowing the harmful ones, clostridia in particular, to multiply and take over. This is called bacterial overgrowth. Clostridia invade the intestinal mucous membrane and produce toxic compounds, which are responsible for the symptoms.

A guinea pig with antibiotic toxicity is depressed, hunched up, anorectic and dehydrated, with abdominal pain and sparse, dry stools or constipation. Gut movements are paralysed, making the abdomen feel flabby. Generally, nothing can be done to cure such a pig. When overgrowth is a reality, nothing seems to be able to stop it. Euthanasia is advisable to prevent further suffering.

To prevent antibiotic toxicity, systemic antibiotics should be used only when necessary. The safest antibiotics possible should be used. Injections are considered safer than oral preparations. Some people consider that the use of a probiotic, e.g. live yoghurt, during antibiotic treatment is useful in restoring healthy flora while others think that it is of no use.

ASTHMA
See Inhalant allergy.

BARBERING
A condition in which loss of coat is caused by fur-chewing.
Hair can be lost in two ways, either if the hair straw falls out by itself or if it is torn out or chewed off. In the case of barbering, the coat is chewed off either by the pig itself or by cagemates.

Barbering may be due to stress, boredom or lack of hay, and there may be a genetic factor as well. Babies may barber their mother if they are hungry while they queue up for a nipple. The longer the coat, the greater the risk of barbering. If a wrapper is too tight, the long-haired guinea pig will chew it off, and cagemates love the long and hay-like coat of a long-haired pig.

Self-barbering is a condition in which a guinea pig chews its own coat. In this case, hairs are removed only in places the pig is able to reach. If a pig chews other pigs, they lose coat more evenly. By observing the pigs and noting which part of the body coat is lost, it will be possible to point out the guilty pig and isolate it. Like other bad habits, barbering is very difficult to cure. However, plenty of space and hay may reduce the problem.

BIRTH INDUCTION
Birth can be induced with hormone injections or be unintended when two pregnant sows share a hutch.

Induction of birth may be tried in case of difficulty in parturition (see Dystocia) or if a sow carries dead babies. Dependent upon whether the sow has an open pelvis or not, different hormones or hormone mixtures can be used.

A special and unwanted kind of birth induction is seen if two pregnant sows share a hutch. When the first sow litters, it is quite normal that the second sow helps with cleaning the newborn babies from foetal membranes and eating the placentas. These structures are full of a hormone, oxytocin, which is intended to produce contractions of the empty uterus and bring down milk for the babies. It may, however, induce delivery in the second sow, who may give birth too early (see Premature babies). Birth contractions may be so severe that the uterus is expelled (see Prolapsed uterus).

BLOAT
Bacterial gas production in the stomach and intestines, which causes distension and pain.

Bloat is mainly seen due to sudden food changes causing disturbances in the intestinal bacterial flora with an overgrowth of gas-producing bacteria. The problem is biggest in the spring, when grass is introduced to the diet, and in the autumn, when kale and cabbage feeding starts.

The main symptoms are a distended abdomen and abdominal pain. The pig may be unaffected or severely affected depending on the degree of distension. Severely affected pigs may die from shock. The distended stomach may also rotate, creating a serious and life-threatening condition (see Gastric dilation and torsion). As gas is present in the form of foam, the guinea pig is unable to excrete the gas. One teaspoonful of vegetable oil reduces surface tension of bubbles, thus destroying the foam and releasing the gas, which passes through the alimentary canal. Preparations for babies against air colic seem efficient as well. Gently massaging the abdomen helps the passage of air. The pig must be kept on a hay and water diet (see Diarrhoea) until normal intestinal function is re-established. In some cases, an antibiotic treatment is recommended too.

'BROKEN BACK'
This describes an area at the centre of the back with hair loss and an open wound.

There are several theories about what causes 'broken back'. There seem to be two distinct syndromes with different causes. The first syndrome is seen in all kinds of pigs and is associated with overheating, i.e. the intake of food items with an excess of energy and protein. Barley, flaked maize and rabbit pellets are suspect in causing overheating. Light-coloured pigs seem more susceptible, and the condition is most common during summertime, especially in hot weather. The same symptoms may be seen in the case of skin parasite infestation where the pig bites itself, often in a V-shaped pattern (see Lice).

The other syndrome is seen during gestation or shortly after parturition. Symptoms are similar and thought to be due to protein and mineral deficiencies during pregnancy.

Treatment includes rinsing of the lesion with sterile saline or a skin antiseptic and an ointment that supports healing. Most 'broken back', however, will heal without treatment. If present, skin parasites must be treated.

CAESAREAN SECTION
This is an operation where babies are delivered through an incision in the womb.

A Caesarean can be performed if a sow is unable to give birth to her babies (see Dystocia) or if she fails to give birth to a dead litter. If the sow is unaffected and not depressed when surgery is performed, her chances are quite good, and, if the babies are alive when removed from the uterus, their chances are good as well. After surgery, the sow must be kept warm and start eating as soon as she wakes from anaesthesia to prevent toxaemia. If the uterus is severely affected, or if the sow is not to be bred from again, it is advisable to surgically remove it (see Ovariohysterectomy). If the sow is depressed and does not eat, her chances of surviving surgery are very poor, and euthanasia will, in most cases, be a better choice.

CANDIDIASIS
A yeast infection with scabs on the lips, especially in lip commissures and harelip.

Candida albicans is a yeast found in small and harmless numbers in the mouth and in the intestinal system. Scabs around the mouth are probably caused by this yeast and are mainly seen in younger pigs. Other factors that contribute to the development of the disease are thought to be acidic food items (such as apples), bacteria and small lesions on the lips. Most cases recover spontaneously due to the development of immunity. However, if the immune system is weak from Vitamin C deficiency, antibiotic treatment or other diseases, the yeast may infect the tongue and oesophagus – a very painful condition that makes the pig salivate and become anorectic. In other pigs, the yeast may invade the internal organs, mainly the lungs and kidneys. This condition is fatal.

CANNIBALISM
The sow mutilates her newborn babies.

Cannibalism as seen in hamsters, where the mother completely eats up several of her young, is not seen in cavies. However, it is quite common to see that stillborn or weak babies are severely bitten. The baby may have lost a leg or the skull may be severely mutilated. This never happens deliberately but may be a reaction to stress, or to prolonged births where the sow has to drag out the baby by her mouth, or when the sow is too eager in her cleaning after birth, or if the sow is young and inexperienced. If bred from again, the sow will rarely repeat her misdeed. There is seen, however, a hereditary lack of maternal quality in some strains of Satins. So, in the case of repeated cannibalism, or if similar problems are known in the strain, such sows should not be bred from again.

CASTRATION
A surgical procedure in boars when the testicles are removed.

Castration is performed on a boar if the owner wants him to go with sows not intended for breeding. But also various testicular diseases, e.g. testicular tumours, are treated through castration. In contrast to many other species, guinea pig boars do not change their behaviour and they continue to mate sows and fight other boars after castration.

CATARACT
A condition in which the lens of the eye turns opaque, causing deteriorated vision or blindness.

There are different kinds of cataract. The most well known is a cataract developing in young adult Abyssinians. The condition is hereditary. However, other unknown factors seem to play a role in the development as well. Congenital cataract may be seen in certain strains of Abyssinians. This is called 'mirror eye'. Cataract is sometimes seen in older pigs, and may be related to diabetes. Finally, opacity develops in pigs with a loose lens (see Lens luxation). This is an incurable disease. Affected pigs, however, seem to do very well, but they should be excluded from breeding and cannot be shown.

CERVICAL LYMPHADENITIS
A contagious disease with abscesses developing on the head or neck.

Many young guinea pigs develop infections in the lymph nodes of the head and neck. The infection is caused by streptococcal bacteria, which are found everywhere in the environment. Symptoms are one or more swellings on the head and neck. These swellings may become very large, but, surprisingly, most pigs remain unaffected. The spread of bacteria leading to septicaemia and death is only rarely seen.

Soon the abscesses mature and may spontaneously open. This is unwanted, as there is a great risk of transmission of bacteria to the cagemates. It is much better to let the veterinarian make an incision and remove the pus as soon as the abscess is mature. The pus is contagious, so the pig must be kept isolated until the wound has healed. Antibiotics are recommended in some cases.

CHEWING
See Barbering.

CHEYLETIELLA
A fur mite that causes pruritus (itching), hair loss and massive amounts of dandruff.

There are many different cheyletiella mites, which prefer different hosts. The guinea pig is infested mainly by the rabbit and the cat mite. Symptoms are mainly seen on the back and rump. Mites inhabit the skin surface but live on tissue fluids and skin, which causes pruritus. The life cycle of the mites varies with temperature and humidity, and they may also be found in the surroundings.

Affected areas show red skin with a thin coat and many large flakes of dandruff. Mites are small and hardly visible. A magnifying glass can be helpful.

Otherwise microscopy of skin scrapings and dandruff is recommended. Cheyletiella mites are susceptible to most antiparasitic preparations. However, it may be necessary to repeat treatments several times and treat surroundings as well.

85

CLUB FOOT
See Pododermatitis.

COCCIDIOSIS
See Intestinal parasites.

CONJUNCTIVITIS
An infection of the mucous membranes on the inside of the eyelids.
   The mucous membranes are red and swollen with excessive lacrimation that may be sticky and cause the eyelids to adhere. The guinea pig is usually otherwise well.
   Conjunctivitis can be caused by several factors. Bacterial infections are quite common. Chemical irritants, such as ammonia build-up in the hutch, aerosols from sprays, dust or foreign bodies caught in the conjunctival sac may also cause conjunctivitis. Chronic conjunctivitis ('red eye') is often caused by allergic conditions such as hay fever or dust allergy. Tooth problems with overgrown tooth roots (see Malocclusion) may cause irritation in the lacrimal duct with ocular discharge as a result. For the treatment of conjunctivitis, the initiating cause must be identified and treated. In the case of dental problems, these must be corrected. Reduction of dust and/or ammonia levels may cause relief. Avoid the use of aerosol sprays in rooms with guinea pigs. Foreign bodies must be removed. Usually an ophthalmic preparation prescribed by the veterinarian is recommended.

CROOKED LEGS
Babies are born with one or both front legs bent due to contraction of the tendons.
   The cause of this condition is unknown, but it may be due to bending of the legs in foetal life. As some breeds (e.g. Self Blacks) are more frequently affected, genetic factors may play a role as well. Affected babies seem happy and are apparently just as mobile as their littermates. But, on closer inspection, it is noticed that one or both front legs are bent so the baby supports itself on the side of the leg, not the foot pad. Sometimes, the condition corrects itself within a couple of weeks, but most legs worsen, and, while weight increases, coat is falling off and the skin thickens at the site of weight support. If a guinea pig is kept as a pet only, it may live a good life providing no complicating skin infections occur. However, for breeding and showing, a guinea pig with crooked legs is useless.

CYSTITIS
This is a bladder infection, causing frequent and painful urination.
The most common symptoms are frequent urination (small amounts each time), whining during urination, and the coat around the vent being wet from urine and blood in the urine. Guinea pigs occasionally excrete a red urine very similar to bloody urine (see Red urine). But no red blood cells are found by microscopy and the pig is unaffected.

Diagnosis is made from clinical signs and urinalysis, where red and white blood cells and sometimes bacteria can be found on microscopy. Cystitis can be caused by crystals and calculi precipitation in the bladder (see Urolithiasis) and radiography may be helpful in diagnosis.

Treatment is by a suitable antibiotic, and, unless calculi are present, the chances for recovery are normally good.

DEMODICOSIS
A skin disease that develops when demodectic mites normally present in hair follicles multiply and destroy hair follicles.
All mammals have demodectic mites in small numbers in their hair follicles. They all belong to the genus demodex and every mammalian species has its own specific demodex species. They are transmitted from mother to suckling offspring shortly after birth. Under normal circumstances, they are kept under control by the immune system, but, in cases of immune suppression (e.g. other diseases or stress), they may get the chance to multiply and become invasive.

Lesions are most commonly seen on the head and around the front legs where hair loss and scabs are seen. Unless secondary skin infection occurs, the condition is not pruritic (itchy).

Diagnosis is made by the veterinarian by identifying demodectic mites from a skin scraping under the microscope. The condition is treated with ivermectin or some other of the avermectins. Treatment must be repeated at 14-day intervals until no mites are found on two subsequent skin scrapings. The immune system must be improved if possible, by eliminating concurrent disease and correct feeding (see Vitamin C deficiency). Only affected animals should be treated.

DENTAL DISEASE
See Malocclusion.

DERMATOPHYTOSIS
A fungal infection in the skin, causing hair loss in patches. Also called ringworm.

Dermatophytosis can be seen in many mammalian species. It is a so-called zoonosis, which means that it can be transmitted to humans as well. The infection is spread through direct contact, or by airborne fungal spores that contaminate the environment. Young animals and children are more susceptible, with adults often immune. Some of the apparently unaffected pigs may act as healthy carriers and pass on infection to youngsters who have not previously been exposed.

Symptoms are seen mainly in the head and neck region and on feet and toes. Symptoms are hair loss and greasy scab formation (see Seborrhoea). Sometimes, mild pruritus (itching) is seen as well. Characteristic lesions are found on the tip of the nose or as a crescent area under the eye, but any part of the skin can be attacked.

Diagnosis is made by microscopy of affected hair and skin scrapings or by culturing the fungus. Dermatophyte species affecting guinea pigs are not fluorescent when lit by a Woods lamp, as many dog and cat dermatophytes are, so this technique is, in this case, useless.

Dermatophytosis may be treated with antifungal dips, shampoos or tablets crushed and mixed into the drinking water, depending upon how many animals there are in the household. All guinea pigs and other mammals should be treated. If contamination in the environment is heavy, they must be treated as well or reinfection may occur. Ask your veterinarian for advice.

In humans, dermatophytosis looks a little different. Common sites are the head, hands and arms, but all parts of the body may be affected. Early lesions are red, slightly swollen, pruritic and clearly marked. Later, they grow in diameter but tend to heal in the centre, giving the characteristic ring-like appearance. This is where the name 'Ringworm' comes from. Treatment with an antifungal ointment is sufficient in most cases.

DIABETES

A disease where lack of insulin leads to weight loss and increased thirst (see Wasting disease).

Insulin is a hormone produced in the pancreatic gland. It is important for transporting glucose (sugar) from the blood through cell membranes into the cells, where it is used as an energy source for all the life processes in a living organism. In the case of diabetes, the pancreatic gland is unable to produce sufficient amounts of insulin. Cells will suffer from lack of glucose for their metabolism. Instead, they must use other and less optimal energy sources, such as fat and protein, which are taken from the body reserves. The guinea pig starts losing weight. In the meantime, when no glucose is consumed by the cells, glucose concentration rises in the blood. In a normal pig, there is no glucose excretion through the kidneys, but when glucose levels in the blood exceed a threshold, the kidneys are unable to withhold glucose, which is excreted in the urine. Therefore, the correct medical term for diabetes is diabetes mellitus, which means 'sugar sweet urine'. When glucose is excreted in urine, the osmotic pressure drags with it lots of water into the urine. To compensate for this, the pig must drink more and more as the disease progresses.

When fat is used as an energy source, some waste products called ketones are produced. One of these is acetone, which is excreted through the lungs and the exhaled air, giving it an acetone smell.

Drinking and wasting is also a common sign when kidneys are unable to concentrate urine (see Kidney failure). Diagnosis of diabetes must therefore be made by blood testing and urinalysis, which shows elevated levels of glucose. There is no insulin treatment available for guinea pigs, but, as long the pig stays happy and alert, there is no reason to euthanase until it looks unwell.

DIARRHOEA
Soft, watery stools, also named 'scours'.

When intestinal function, in one way or another, is compromised, diarrhoea is often the result. Guinea pigs are unable to vomit, so whatever is ingested has to pass all the way through. Most causes of diarrhoea are dietetic, i.e. are caused by the food. The intestinal microflora is important for normal function of the digestive system, but the balance is delicate, so minor changes in the intestinal environment may kill useful micro-organisms and favour the multiplication of harmful ones. Common dietary causes of diarrhoea are feeding with frosty or mouldy food, sudden food changes and feeding grass clippings. Some children find it amusing to offer sweets and other unsuitable food items, which can cause diarrhoea. Feeding many juicy greens with a laxative effect may produce softer stools, which will stop when the amounts are reduced.

Symptoms in dietary diarrhoea vary from very mild to alarming and acute symptoms, such as severe abdominal pain, distended intestines (see Bloat), considerable fluid loss, electrolyte disturbances, depression and sudden death. Mildly affected pigs can be treated by dietary adjustments only. The pig is placed on a hay and water diet only (maybe a small piece of cucumber daily, as it is virtually 100 per cent water and as such is a good fluid source) for three to five days. When stools are normalised, a slow and gradual introduction of other food items can be made. Identification of the cause is often impossible, but, to avoid recurrence, only fresh, good-quality food items should be fed. More severe cases must be treated by a veterinarian. Possible medications include analgesics (pain killers), antibiotics, and fluid replacement therapy. If the pig is severely affected and anorectic, many cases will be fatal.

There are many other causes of diarrhoea apart from dietetic. These are dealt with elsewhere (see Enteritis, Intestinal parasites, and Antibiotic toxicity).

'DRINKING AND WASTING'
See Wasting disease.

DYSTOCIA
A condition where the sow is unable to give birth to her babies.
This is a common and very serious condition in the guinea pig. Causes may be rigid symphysis in the pelvis because the sow is too old for her first litter or because she has been rested for too long between litters (see chapter seven), making it impossible for babies to pass through the pelvic canal. Other causes may be too narrow a pelvic canal in very young sows, babies too large (e.g. in a single-baby pregnancy), malpositioned or malformed babies, weakness from pregnancy toxaemia, or malnutrition.

A sow with dystocia will strain without producing any young. In the beginning, straining is almost continuous, but later, it is more intermittent as the sow gets exhausted. Soon the sow will become depressed and have a brownish vaginal discharge. Complications in this stage are very common (see Pregnancy toxaemia, and Metritis). Left untreated, the sow will die.

If the sow is still straining and relatively unaffected, the baby may be extracted using fingers or forceps. This is usually a job for a veterinarian. If unsuccessful, an injection stimulating birth contractions may help. Sometimes, labour may also be stimulated by holding the sow's rear end in lukewarm water. If there are still no results, the babies must be removed by surgery (see Caesarean section).

ECLAMPSIA
A calcium deficiency causing twitches in suckling sows.
The condition is relatively rare. It is seen predominantly in older sows suckling a large litter, and develops up to one week after

parturition. The sow becomes depressed and has twitches. In later stages, convulsions may develop. In early stages, a calcium injection may reverse symptoms, but, in later stages, treatment is unsuccessful.

The disease can be prevented by feeding calcium-rich greens and vegetables during pregnancy and lactation. Grass and dandelion leaves are good calcium sources in the summer season, while carrots and beetroot are useful during the winter.

ENTERITIS
An infection in the intestinal tract. The most consistent symptom is diarrhoea.

Bacterial and viral diarrhoeas are infrequently seen. Sometimes, they are transmitted by mice and rats, but more commonly, enteritis is caused by bacterial overgrowth. In this case, harmful bacteria present in small numbers in the intestinal tract for some reason start multiplying, leading to severe changes in the intestinal environment (see Diarrhoea, and Antibiotic toxicity). Poor cage hygiene, nutritional deficiencies (see Vitamin C deficiency), stress and overcrowding may predispose the animal to overgrowth of such potentially harmful germs. The most common bacterial causes of enteritis are salmonella, yersinia, Escherichia coli and clostridia. The former two can be transmitted to humans (see Zoonoses).

Symptoms are very similar no matter which bacteria are involved. The onset may be acute, with diarrhoea, sometimes bloody or slimy. Depression, anorexia and dehydration are other common symptoms.

 Death is seen within a couple of days. Sudden deaths with no preceding symptoms are also seen. Some pigs may develop more chronic symptoms, such as weight loss, failure to thrive, and sometimes death within a couple of weeks. Surviving guinea pigs may act as latent carriers, which can transmit disease to babies and unexposed adults.

Exact diagnosis can be made by microbial examination of stools and by post-mortem studies. The bacteria should be examined for antibiotic sensitivity for therapeutic purposes. However, in many cases, treatment is inadvisable. In case of zoonosis, the animal should be culled, as it is a potential health hazard to humans. Moreover, it is undesirable to create healthy disease carriers, so again culling is a reasonable solution.

If treatment is attempted, sick animals must be isolated and treated with an antibiotic, according to the sensitivity test. Fluid therapy, corticosteroids, vitamins and other supportive therapies may also be beneficial. Predisposing factors should be eliminated to avoid recurrence, and a thorough cleaning and disinfection of the shed should be carried out before reintroducing animals. Contaminated bedding and stools should be burned.

ENTROPION
The cause is an in-turning eyelid where eyelashes cause irritation and ulceration of the cornea.
See also Keratitis.

EPIDERMOID CYST
A node in the skin containing a thick paste-like greyish material.
   This is the most common tumour in the guinea pig, and, fortunately, it is benign. It is formed by a clogged-up hair follicle and the content is a mixture of sebum and dead skin cells. When squeezing the tumour, the thick but soft content can be felt.

   Epidermoid cysts are very common in older pigs and are found mainly on the back and rump. Even though they can become very large, it does not seem to bother the pig. Therefore, such a cyst can be left in most cases.

   If the cyst bursts, the paste-like, greyish-white contents can be squeezed out and the cyst afterwards rinsed by an antiseptic solution. If the cyst fills up again, it may be necessary to remove it surgically, but only if the pig is hampered by it.

EUTHANASIA
This is another word for putting an animal to sleep.
   It is often difficult to talk about euthanasia, because it is such an emotional subject. The owner wants a sick guinea pig cured, but many times this is just not possible. In the case of dental disease (see Malocclusion), euthanasia is often recommended, but many other fatal or incurable diseases justify euthanasia. The owner, or – if the owner is under age – the parents of the owner, must take the responsibility to avoid unnecessary suffering by wishing the best for the animal and not for themselves. Euthanasia should be performed by a veterinarian and is not dramatic at all. An overdose of an anaesthetic preparation is injected and the guinea pig dies in its sleep.

EXTRA TOES
See Polydactyly.

'FATTY EYE'
A pink swelling protruding under the lower eyelid.
   The condition is due to a swelling in the conjunctival sac, causing a hanging lower eyelid. The condition cannot be cured but luckily the pig is otherwise unaffected. Because of its hereditary nature, affected pigs should be excluded from breeding. 'Fatty eye' is a show disqualification.

FLYSTRIKE
See Myiasis.

FOOT ABSCESS
See Abscesses, and Pododermatitis.

GASTRIC DILATION AND TORSION
A serious condition where the stomach overfills with fluid and air (dilation) and sometimes rotates as well (torsion).
   The cause of gastric dilation and torsion is unknown, but propagating gas-producing bacteria may be responsible in some cases (see Bloat). Overfilling of the stomach may also contribute as well as hereditary factors. If treated with an unsuitable antibiotic, the overgrowth of gas-producing bacteria may be favoured (see Antibiotic toxicity) A commercial dry food has been connected with gastric dilation and torsion, but so far nothing has been proved.
   Symptoms are unspecific, with depression and anorexia being the first signs; maybe a distended abdomen is observed. Sudden death without preceding signs is quite common. The diagnosis is made at post-mortem examination. There is no known effective treatment.

GUINEA PIG PARALYSIS
See Hind limb paralysis.

HAY MITES
Tiny mites that live off dandruff, grease and skin debris. They are located in the coat, mainly on the rump.
   Although not a variety of louse, these mites are commonly known under the name 'static lice', as opposed to 'running lice' (see Lice). The scientific name is *Chirodiscoides cavia*. A single hay mite is hardly visible to the naked eye, but, in case of heavier infestations where they are found in abundance, they are easily seen, especially on the rump. The colour is greyish and thus more visible in dark and white pigs, where

93

they can completely destroy the overall appearance. They tend to sit on the mid-section of the hair straw, and, unless looked at very closely for some time, they do not seem to move. At shows, hay mites are regarded as a fault if the overall appearance is disturbed, but they are not a show disqualification.

There is some dispute about where hay mites come from. Some claim that they come from the hay (hence the name), while others regard them as specific guinea pig parasites and claim that they should be treated as such. As they are not intrusive and live on hair straws with only little contact with the skin, the vast majority of pigs are unaffected by the presence of hay mites.

Treatment is quite difficult. Hay mites are not susceptible to many of the common antiparasitic preparations, and resistance develops readily. However, it is often possible to reduce the numbers considerably, especially if a combination of preparations is used. This may lead to over-dosage, as one preparation may potentiate the effect of the other and it is important to consider whether the cure is worse than the disease. As a consequence, many fanciers only treat pigs that go to shows.

However, one health problem may occur. Some pigs seem to become sensitised to mites such as dust mites and hay mites, and become pruritic (see Skin allergy, and Seborrhoea). Such pigs must be kept as free from dust and static lice as possible, and glucocorticoid treatments may sometimes prove useful.

HEART ATTACK
See 'Sudden death'.

HEAT STROKE

A life-threatening condition due to overheating.

Guinea pigs are quite susceptible to high temperatures. At 28 degrees Celsius (82.4 degrees Fahrenheit) or above, there is a great risk of heat stroke. A transport box in a car boot may become a very hot place in the summer, and many pigs have died from heat stroke under these conditions. Of course, leaving a guinea pig in a parked car in the sun is highly irresponsible. Many sheds become very hot during summer. Good ventilation is a must.

A guinea pig with heat stroke is inactive, flaccid, and hyperventilates with an open mouth. The body temperature is high, exceeding 40 degrees Celsius (104 degrees Fahrenheit). If not cooled down quickly, collapse and death is likely to occur. A guinea pig with heat stroke should be cooled down with cool (not ice-cold) water and left in a quiet, well-ventilated place for air-drying. Cooling may be repeated if necessary.

HIND LIMB PARALYSIS

The hind legs are paralysed. The guinea pig drags itself forwards by the front legs while the hind legs are floppy and dragged behind the pig.

The most common cause for hind limb paralysis is a fall. Guinea pigs are creatures living on the ground and are not built for falling down from heights. Small children particularly can very easily drop a guinea pig, often resulting in fracture of the spine and spinal cord damage. This leads to hind limb paralysis, from which it is highly unlikely to recover. Such pigs must be euthanased as soon as the veterinarian has made the diagnosis, as the pig is likely to be in pain.

Other causes are nutritional (see Vitamin C deficiency, and Vitamin D toxicity). A virus causing guinea pig paralysis has been described, but is thought to be very rare.

HORMONAL ALOPECIA

Hair loss induced under the influence of sex hormones in pregnant or post partum sows, in sows with ovarian cysts or in newborns and weanlings.

Hormones affect the function of hair follicles and may bring them to a state where they cease to function and hair growth stops. When a hair is shed, it is not replaced and the guinea pig's coat becomes thin. This is most pronounced on the flanks and lower abdomen, and, typical for hormonal alopecia, hair loss is symmetrical and no pruritus is observed.

Alopecia in pregnant sows is seen in the last trimester of gestation and is more common in older sows who have been frequently bred. Without treatment, hair will grow out after parturition. A supplement of vitamin B is thought to support regrowth. The condition is likely to reappear in subsequent pregnancies. The same symptoms may be seen in sows shortly after parturition; again the condition resolves spontaneously. Many older sows have cystic ovaries (see Ovarian cysts). These cysts are producing hormones and may cause symmetric alopecia over the flanks as well as other symptoms.

On rare occasions, maternal hormones during gestation and parturition may cause alopecia in newborn babies. Shortly after birth, they start losing coat but remain happy and eat well. The coat will soon grow out again without further treatment.

Weanlings may get a thin hair coat when they lose their baby coat. This is considered perfectly normal and has nothing to do with hormonal alopecia.

HYPERKERATOTIC FOOT PADS
A piece of hard, dead skin is formed on the foot pad, looking like an extra toe.

This is seen more commonly in older pigs on the front legs. Sometimes, the dead skin curls around. It can easily be clipped off, and, as it is dead, no blood vessels or nerves are present.

IMPACTED RECTUM
A condition seen mainly in older boars where the rectum becomes loose and caecotrophs accumulate.

Most older boars have a more or less impacted rectum. From the outside it is noticed that the anus is distended and filled with a brownish-grey, foul-smelling material. The impaction consists of the soft stools, the caecotrophs (see chapter seven). The normal hard droppings are usually able to pass the impaction. An impacted rectum is a permanent incurable condition, and the anus must be normally emptied once or twice a week for the rest of the guinea pig's life.

Another kind of impaction is seen in the anal sac, which is situated between the anus and the genital opening. The anal sac has many scent glands, which are used to attract sows. Again, older boars are most commonly affected. The impaction consists of skin debris and secretions from the scent glands in the anal sac and has an unpleasant smell. Again, the contents can be emptied at regular intervals.

INFERTILITY IN BOARS
The boar fails to make sows pregnant.

Infertility has many causes in the boar. Stress and obesity seem to decrease fertility. Semen quality may be decreased due to infection, hormonal imbalances or testicular tumours, the penis or prepuce may be malformed or the boar may have lost his libido. Vitamin C and E deficiency may also be considered.

A boar with suspected infertility should have his penis, prepuce and testicles examined. Normally the boar has two horny spikes at the tip of the penis. If one or both are absent, or if they are of unequal lengths, these may be signs of infertility. A loose prepuce may predispose for a protruding penis (see Paraphimosis) and infection. The testicles should be symmetric and without swellings and pain.

Boars may lose libido (i.e. suffer from decreased sex drive). This is seen in obese boars and boars who have not been bred from before they are one year old. For inexperienced boars it may take some time to perform a proper mating. This should not be confused with infertility.

INFERTILITY IN SOWS
The sow is unable to become pregnant.

This may be due to malnutrition (e.g. vitamin C or E deficiency), obesity, infection in the genital organs (see Metritis), ovarian disease (see Ovarian cysts), stress, over-showing, dead desiccated foetuses (see Mummification), old age or having been bred too much. Many sows are slow breeders in the winter if they receive daylight only, as light triggers sex hormone production. Sometimes, a sow refuses to let a particular boar mate her. Many cases of infertility can be cured, providing the cause is identified and corrected.

INHALANT ALLERGY
Allergy caused by inhaled particles, where symptoms come from the upper and/or lower airways.

Guinea pigs live in dust-filled environments with hay and shavings. If they are kept indoors, they may also be irritated by different aerosols. All these things may cause an allergy, and symptoms may appear from the upper airways, such as a running nose, sneezing or mucosal swelling (see Ruttling).

More serious are allergies in the lower airways, because mucus is produced in excessive amounts and the small bronchi are contracting (asthma). This causes laboured breathing and sometimes death. The diagnosis is made by a veterinarian by clinical examination and radiography, and treatment should be a combination of eliminating dust and aerosols, and possibly the administration of glucocorticoid to decrease symptoms.

INTESTINAL PARASITES
Parasites living their adult life inside the intestines, which may cause diarrhoea and failure to thrive.

Intestinal parasites in the guinea pig are divided into worms and protozoa (one-celled organisms). Worms are infrequently seen, and most worms do not seem to have guinea pigs as their natural hosts but are transmitted when feeding contaminated grass. The worm *Parasporidia uncinata* is the most commonly seen. It lives in the caecum and is about 1-3 cm (0.4-1.2 inches) long. Tapeworms and roundworms are rare. The symptoms are similar. Most pigs show no signs at all, but, in cases of heavy infestation, weight loss, retarded growth, diarrhoea or constipation is seen.

Diagnosis is made by identifying worm eggs in a faecal sample and treatment is an antiparasitic preparation according to which worm is diagnosed. Thorough cleaning of the hutch and improved hygiene is essential in avoiding a recurrence.

Protozoa are sometimes seen. Coccidia are the most commonly recognised. They are found in small numbers in the intestinal flora, but due to stress, other diseases, malnutrition or poor hygiene, disease may occur. Coccidia have a life stage outside the host, which takes a minimum of seven days under optimal conditions, and, if hutches are only cleaned at longer intervals, contamination may build up in the environments.

The symptoms are bloody and slimy diarrhoea, retarded growth and failure to thrive. Diagnosis is made on microscopy of faecal samples or at post-mortem examination. Treatment should be accompanied by improved hygiene. Other protozoa are rarely seen and are associated with the suppression of the immune system.

IN-TURNING EYELIDS
See Entropion, and Juvenile Keratitis.

IVERMECTIN
A useful drug that can be used against most parasitic infestations.
This drug belongs to the group of avermectins. Ivermectin is the most commonly used drug in the avermectin group, as it is well tolerated and has been used in thousands of pigs with excellent results over the years. A new derivative, selamectin, is promising for the future. The drug works by irreversibly binding neurotransmitters in the parasites' nervous system leading to paralysis. Fortunately, mammal nervous systems work differently, so avermectins are relatively non-toxic.

Ivermectin can be given orally (by mouth) or by injections. These should be performed by a veterinarian, as a faulty injection technique may lead to inflammation, hair loss and permanent bald patches. To eliminate all stages in the parasite life cycle effectively, the treatment should be repeated. Ask your veterinarian for further advice.

JUVENILE KERATITIS

This is an eye condition involving corneal opacity and is seen in newborn babies.

Juvenile keratitis is quite common but usually benign. It may be seen in one or both eyes. Babies are otherwise unaffected. Newborns, or babies aged a few days old, develop corneal milky opacity. Guinea pigs open their eyes when they are still in the womb, and at this stage they may get eyelashes into the eye, causing irritation and oedema (swelling) of the cornea, making it opaque. Certain breeds, i.e. the Texel, are predisposed to inward-turning eyelashes.

Treatment includes removing the eyelashes from the eye. If they constantly stick to the eye, it is advisable to pluck them out. When they grow again, they usually cause no problems. The eye and surroundings can be gently cleaned with sterile saline twice a day. Usually the condition clears within few days. Antibiotic eye preparations are only necessary for complicated cases.

In cases of permanent in-turning eyelashes (see Entropion), a minor operation will correct the condition. Such animals should not be used for breeding, as it may be hereditary.

KERATITIS

Keratitis is an inflammation in the cornea, i.e. the translucent membrane that covers and protects the eye.

The causes of keratitis are numerous, but most frequently it is due to a foreign body. Guinea pigs often get a shaving, a seed or a piece of hay into the eye. It often does not seem to bother them at all, but in due course it will cause irritation and damage to the cornea, which will become milky and opaque. The guinea pig will screw up its eye and an ocular discharge may be seen. Occasionally, an ulcer is visible. In chronic cases, blood vessels start growing into the cornea providing nourishment for the healing process. These usually disappear when healing is completed.

Keratitis is certainly a case for the vet. First of all, the eye must be thoroughly examined, as the foreign body may still be stuck under the

eyelid. Unless it is removed, there will be no healing. An antibiotic eye preparation should also be used. If left untreated, there is a risk of permanent damage to the eye (i.e. in the form of scar formation), or, if a foreign body penetrates the cornea, a panophthalmitis (an infection affecting all structures of the eye) will destroy the eye, causing blindness and eyeball collapse.

KIDNEY FAILURE
A disease in which reduced kidney function leads to loss of protein and water through the urine, causing drinking and wasting (see Wasting disease).

Kidney failure is a disease that is slowly progressive, and kidney damage usually starts long before symptoms become evident. The kidneys have a very large reserve capacity, so it is not until about 75 per cent of the kidney tissue has been destroyed that it becomes unable to excrete waste products, such as urea.

Many factors may be responsible for kidney destruction. Chronic bacterial or viral infections are some of them. Hereditary factors may also play a role. Feeding food items with a high phosphorus content (i.e. sunflower seeds, nuts and peas) has been associated with the development of kidney disease. Finally, a toxic matter named ochratoxine, which is produced by fungal organisms in mouldy hay and grain, is known to damage kidney tissue.

Kidney damage means that pores in the kidney tissue, which normally are too small for protein molecules to pass through, enlarge and allow through a small protein called albumin. Because protein is lost through the urine, demand for protein from food increases. However, when protein loss exceeds protein intake, the guinea pig starts losing its own body protein, i.e. mainly muscles. This is seen as a weight loss where hips and shoulders start protruding. The kidneys also lose the ability to withhold water, so the pig urinates more and must drink more to avoid dehydration. When more kidney tissue is lost, the kidneys become unable to excrete waste products, such as urea, by protein metabolism. This means that urea builds up in the blood, causing the poisoning of the pig. Until this stage, the pig will have been happy and alert, but urea poisoning causes depression and finally death.

Symptoms are identical to those caused by elevated levels of glucose in the urine (see Diabetes), so only an analysis of blood and urinary samples can reveal a diagnosis. In the case of kidney failure, the gravity of the urine is very low and has a high protein content. There is no cure for kidney failure – lost kidney tissue cannot be replaced. Kidney destruction and the disease's progress may be delayed by reducing phosphorous intake and increasing protein in the diet, but, unlike with dogs and cats, there are no kidney diets available for guinea pigs.

LENS LUXATION

The lens loses its firm attachment and falls down in the posterior eye chamber. Vision is partly or completely lost.

Lens luxation may be a hereditary condition, since certain breeds are more susceptible, i.e. Peruvians. One or both eyes may be affected. However, there is often a history of a sudden onset of the condition after transportation or being chased around by other pigs, so trauma seems to be another part of the disease. Lens luxation is untreatable. However, most pigs seem happy and eat well. Pigs with lens luxation should not be bred from.

LICE

Small, wingless insects on the skin surface that live off grease and skin debris.

The most common parasites in the guinea pig are called 'running lice', as opposed to 'static lice' (see hair mites). They spend all the time on the skin surface. Eggs are fastened at the hair base. Guinea pig lice are not blood-suckers, but live on debris, and, as a consequence, do not cause an intensive pruritus. They are host-specific, i.e. they live on guinea pigs and guinea pigs only. At shows, guinea pigs with lice are disqualified.

Symptoms depend upon how heavily infested the pig is. Many pigs seem to live for years with only a few lice and no other symptoms. However, if the pig gets sick or stressed, the immune system may be compromised so that the lice are able to multiply. Some pigs seem to develop louse allergy and show mild to moderate pruritus, especially in the centre of the back. The pig bites itself and a V-shaped area of hair loss on the mid-back, describing the front border that is reachable with its teeth, is commonly seen.

The most common guinea pig louse is called *Gliricola porcelli*. It is a yellowish-white, worm-like insect about 1 mm (0.04 inches) long, which wriggles around between hairs, mainly on the back and rump, trying to escape from the light. It is more visible on dark coats. Lice are very easy to treat with any antiparasitic preparation. Another treatment, given a week later, may be necessary. Ask your veterinarian for advice. All guinea pigs in the household must be treated.

LYMPHOSARCOMA

Cancer in the lymph nodes, which become hard and swollen.

If the lymph nodes are swollen in several places around the body, it is likely that the guinea pig suffers from lymph node cancer, lymphosarcoma. All, or multiple, lymph nodes have been attacked by malignant lymph cells that spread readily through the blood. It is an incurable disease as it is extensive before it is diagnosed, and because chemotherapy for guinea pigs is not available. Diagnosis is made from the symptoms and examination of cells taken from a lymph node. Euthanasia should be performed if the pig suffers and loses weight.

MALOCCLUSION
A dental disease where the teeth overgrow and prevent the guinea pig from eating.

Problems with overgrown teeth are very common in guinea pigs. The teeth of guinea pigs are continuously growing. The wear of the teeth must correspond with the growth, or the teeth become too long. Malocclusion can afflict the incisors, the molars or both. Most commonly, the primary problem is molar malocclusion leading to a secondary incisor malocclusion. It is a multifactorial disease, which means that it is a combination of several factors that decide whether a pig develops dental problems or not.

Some of those factors are genetic, but other causes include malnutrition (see Vitamin C deficiency), tooth trauma, tooth infection, old age, or the provision of non-abrasive food. Strong genetic predisposition means that malocclusion will develop at a young age (1 year or before) no matter how perfect the feeding is. A smaller degree of genetic predisposition may not show because other factors are not present, or not until the pig is old. Congenital malocclusion is seen in white babies with small or no eyes (see Microphthalmia).

The most important symptom is gradual weight loss despite alertness and great interest in the food. However, food preferences seem to alter from hard to softer food items as malocclusion progresses. Chewing becomes slower and a grating sound may be heard. Some pigs simply drop food out of their mouths. Weight loss is quicker if the pig has a cagemate who will eat all the food. Finally the guinea pig stops eating. At this point, it often has diarrhoea due to a lack of intestinal fibre and vitamin C deficiency, and it is extremely thin.

Diagnosis should be made from inspection of the incisors and the oral cavity. The latter is impossible without special instruments and deep sedation. When molars are maloccluded, the mouth is permanently wide open and the incisors become overlong as well.

When molars overgrow, the mandible is forced forward, placing the lower incisors just beneath the upper instead of slightly behind. At this point, the incisors lose their chisel shape because they are unable to sharpen each other any more. The first lower molars are now positioned in front of the corresponding upper molars. Hence there is no wear of the lower ones, which overgrow. Because of the angling of the teeth, the lower molars grow towards and over the tongue, entrapping it and preventing the guinea pig from swallowing in a normal way.

When the mouth is opened to its maximum, the teeth cannot continue growing into the oral cavity. Instead, they may start growing inwards, causing overlong tooth roots that can eventually break through the bone and into the nasal sinus or to the eye (upper molars), or through the mandibular bone (lower molars). Tooth abscesses are infrequently seen (contrary to the rabbit), but when present may be associated with tooth root overgrowth.

Occasionally, tooth spikes are seen. These are small, very sharp spurs formed by the uneven wear of the molars. Spikes on the lower molars protrude into the tongue and may cause tongue lesions. Spikes on the upper molars are directed into the cheek. These do not seem to be as painful, but may cause infection and abscesses.

Guinea pigs with malocclusion are virtually impossible to treat, because many of them are presented to the veterinarian in a very bad state and far too late. To examine the pig properly, it must be sedated and anaesthetized. The oral cavity must be inspected, and overgrowth and spikes must be corrected. Radiography of the teeth and jaws is necessary to access potential tooth root overgrowth and the state of the mandibular joint.

If a single spike, or a few, are found in a pig in reasonable condition, the chances are good. Most other pigs, however, cannot be treated efficiently and eventually they die. Emaciated pigs, those with tooth root overgrowth, and those with permanently distended mouths although tooth correction has been carried out (due to permanent damage to the mandibular joint) are better euthanased, as they are unlikely to survive. Force-feeding for selfish purposes prolongs the suffering of the pig (see Euthanasia).

In those few cases when treatment is successful, everything must be done to prevent recurrence. Feeding more abrasive food, grass, and other greens, plus hay and small branches from fruit trees, works well. Dry food must be guinea pig pellets with vitamin C supplementation. In particular, oily seeds, nuts and dried peas should not be fed. If there is any likelihood that the condition is hereditary, parents who produce youngsters with dental problems should be excluded from breeding.

MAMMARY GLAND TUMOURS
A hard, painless swelling of tumorous origin in a mammary gland.
Mammary gland tumours are quite common in guinea pigs, in boars as well as sows. A hard lump in the mammary gland of a non-suckling sow or a boar is likely to be a mammary gland tumour. The gland is not sore but, frequently, there is a watery or blood-stained discharge from the nipple. Most mammary gland tumours are benign and slow-growing, and the guinea pig seems unaffected, even in cases of large tumours. From time to time, mammary gland tumours get infected and repeated antibiotic treatments may be necessary. Surgical removal is the treatment of choice and recurrence is unlikely to occur. However, if the guinea pig is old and unaffected by the tumour, many owners prefer to avoid surgery and leave it in place. Frequently, such a pig dies from old age without being affected by the tumour.

MANGE
A skin disease caused by a burrowing mite, which triggers severe itching.
The disease is caused by a tiny mite called *Trixacarus cavia*, which is closely related to the itch mite in humans. It is also called Sellnick, named after the first person who identified and described it. The life cycle is rather complicated and involves a female tunnelling into the skin where she lays her eggs, causing intense pruritus (itching). When the eggs are hatched, the young mites migrate to the surface of the skin. At this stage they are called nymphs. They mature into adult males and females. Mating occurs on the skin surface and then the female starts burrowing. The time span from egg to adult fertile mite is two to three weeks.

The first signs of disease are usually a thinning of coat, with dandruff and slight pruritus. Initial symptoms occur predominantly in the groin, on the shoulders, and around the neck and the front legs. Later, pruritus and skin irritation increases. The guinea pig bites and scratches itself. Such self-traumatising leads to open sores. In the later stages, the skin all over the body is affected, with hair loss, thick, greasy and yellowish scabs (see Seborrhoea) and infected wounds. Weight loss is also seen. In late stages, the guinea pig is tortured by pruritus, unable to eat or sleep. Handling aggravates pruritus and even good-natured pigs may bite when handled. Pruritus may also cause convulsions, which have great similarities to epileptic seizures. If untreated, the pig will finally die.

Symptoms may occur only a few weeks after infection, but many guinea pigs will stay symptomless, sometimes for several years. However, they will be acting as healthy carriers of the disease. In cases of stress, e.g. pregnancy, changes in the environment, other concurrent diseases or old age, the mites will start multiplying and symptoms will occur. For this reason, symptoms in a large stock of guinea pigs can vary, with no indication at all of severely affected pigs about to die from the disease, or any stage of the disease in between.

The veterinarian will make the diagnosis from clinical signs and microscopy of skin scrapings. After a group of drugs called avermectins (see Ivermectin) were introduced, treatment of guinea pig mange has become easy and efficient, and almost all animals, no matter how severely affected, will recover. The guinea pig receives two treatments, 10 to 14 days apart. After a few hours, it will stop scratching, wounds will heal, scabs will dry out and fall off, and new hairs will grow. The pig will quickly gain weight again.

All pigs in a household should be treated. Humans and other animals are not infected. Mange is acutely life-threatening in pregnant sows (see Pregnancy toxaemia), as they may develop toxaemia without any, or with only very few, visible skin symptoms. If many pregnant sows in stock develop toxaemia, mange should always be suspected. Therefore, it is important to treat all pigs, and not exclude the pregnant ones. The risk for the sow is much bigger if left untreated.

MASTITIS
An infection in a mammary gland.

Mastitis is seen in suckling sows and in mammary gland tumours. The sow has only two nipples, so, when she has a large litter, this means that the babies have to queue up to wait for milk. Many hungry babies may cause damage to the nipple, allowing bacterial intrusion. The mammary gland becomes red, hard, swollen and sore. Secretions may become bloodstained or thick and yellow. The formation of abscesses is sometimes seen. The sow may or may not become depressed.

Treatment depends upon the symptoms. If the sow is still eating and well, she may be cured by just giving her hot water compresses and milking out the gland a couple of times a day, leaving her with her babies the rest of the time. If the sow is depressed, she must be brought to a veterinarian, who will consider an antibiotic treatment. Babies must be removed and hand-reared or be given a foster mum. If many sows in stock get mastitis, hygiene must be improved and a bacterial culture must be performed to find a suitable antibiotic.

METRITIS
A uterine infection, most often seen after abortion or birth.
The sow has a vaginal discharge with blood and/or pus and quite often she is depressed and anorectic. She may develop pregnancy toxaemia as well. The sow must be treated by a vet with antibiotics and supportive therapy. Sometimes surgery (see Ovariohysterectomy) may be performed. If many sows in a colony get ill from metritis, a post-mortem and microbiological examination may help find the cause.

Sometimes a symptomless metritis is found in sows unable to become pregnant (see Infertility in sows), but very little is known about it. A disease called cystic endometritis is occasionally seen in non-pregnant sows. Symptoms are bleeding from uterus (see Uterine bleeding) with a bloody vaginal discharge.

MICROPHTHALMIA
Babies are white and born with diminutive pink eyes.
This is caused by a lethal gene existing in Roan- and Dalmation-marked guinea pigs. Pigs with a single Roan/Dalmation gene have the desired marking; however, when mating a Roan/Dalmation with another Roan/Dalmation, about one in four babies will carry the lethal gene in double dose and it will show its effect.

The babies are microphthalmic or anophthalmic (without eyes), white and often with deformed teeth. Most of them are born dead or die a few hours after birth. If not, they usually die shortly after weaning because the deformed teeth prevent them from eating solid food. Breeders should be very aware of the dangers of breeding pigs with Roan/Dalmation genes together, and must inform buyers about the risk.

MIDDLE EAR INFECTION
See Otitis media.

MOUTH SCABS
See Candidiasis.

MUMMIFICATION
A dead foetus that becomes shrivelled and is maintained in the uterus.

Sometimes, when a foetus dies, it does not induce an abortion but stays in the uterus for a shorter or longer period. If other foetuses continue to develop, the mummified foetus is usually delivered at term with the babies. It is small, brown and dry with a hollow instead of an eye. In the case of a single-foetus pregnancy, the mummified foetus may persist and be a cause of infertility. Such a foetus can usually be diagnosed by feeling it through the abdominal wall or by radiography. Surgery is often needed to remove it.

MYCOSIS
See Dermatophytosis, Skin mycoses, and Candidiasis.

MYIASIS
Blowflies lay their eggs in open wounds or on skin irritated and soiled by diarrhoea or urine. The hatched larvae create severe tissue damage and shock.

Normally, blowflies lay their eggs in meat and carcasses, but sometimes they become attracted by the smell of infected and open wounds, or skin soiled by soft stools or urine. The hatched larvae are called maggots and they dig into the skin and underlying tissue, causing severe inflammation and necrotic (dead) tissue. The pig becomes severely affected and will die from shock if untreated. However, guinea pigs do not seem as susceptible as rabbits.

Diagnosis is easy once the maggots are seen. The veterinarian will treat the condition by removing all visible maggots, perform a proper wound and antibiotic treatment, and kill all remaining maggots with ivermectin or a related compound (see Ivermectin). The success rate is good, except in cases of large areas of tissue necrosis and shock.

ORPHAN BABIES
Babies that cannot suckle their mother.

If a sow is lost during or within a few days following birth, or if she has no milk (see Agalactia) or infection in the mammary gland (see Mastitis), babies must be reared by a foster mother or by hand. Finding a foster mum, e.g. one who lost her babies or had only one or two in her litter, is the best and easiest solution. Most sows with very young babies will accept orphans. It may be necessary to move such a mother into a small box without her own young for a couple of hours to allow the new babies to acclimatise and get the smell of the sow. The foster mum will reject the babies if they are too weak to suckle and follow her.

If no foster mother is available, hand-rearing is the only alternative. Commercial baby food, such as porridge containing milk and fruit, is excellent for hand-rearing. It contains cereals that are more substantial than milk alone, making nightly feedings unnecessary. As guinea pig babies usually eat solid food from day one, they are not so dependent upon a milk-only diet.

Babies should be fed through a dropper or a syringe every second to third hour during the day. Allow them to drink some water afterwards. Give them as much porridge as they can consume without force-feeding, as many babies die from aspiration of force-fed food into the lungs. Babies too weak to swallow are unlikely to survive.

Clean around the mouth with a piece of damp cotton wool (cotton) after feeding, and do not forget to clean around the anus as well. This will stimulate urination and defecation. Do not expect all babies to survive. The survival rate is about 50 per cent, with the biggest, most hungry and more active babies having better chances. Dry food, hay and greens (preferably grass) should be available at all times to encourage the babies to start eating. Hand-rearing should be continued for two to three weeks.

Babies will be happy to have company. A gentle boar, or a retired sow who used to be a good and caring mother, will accept and nurse the babies and allow them to hide under them. This gives babies a will to live and increases the survival rate. Hand-reared babies will develop a woolly and unhealthy-looking coat, but a normal coat will grow when they lose their baby coat.

OSTEOPOROSIS
See Vitamin D toxicity.

OTITIS MEDIA
An infection in the middle ear, which may lead to head tilt.
A major sign is disturbances of the sense of balance, which is located in the middle ear. The head will tilt to the affected side, and the guinea pig may circle around or fall on its side. Despite that, many pigs seem relatively unaffected and eat well. However, otitis is sometimes seen as a complication to pneumonia, and such pigs are usually depressed. Some pigs have otitis media without showing any signs, but have the disease diagnosed as an incidental finding at post mortem.

Radiography is the only reliable diagnosis. There is no therapy available to cure the disease. Damage to balance is usually irreversible, but a single pet may be able to live a decent life despite its disability.

Affected pigs from a colony should be euthanased because of the infection risk.

OVARIAN CYSTS
Fluid-filled cysts on the ovaries that may cause infertility and hair loss.

The incidence of ovarian cysts is thought to be quite high, especially in older sows where up to 90 per cent have been found to have cysts in one or both ovaries at post mortem examinations. The reason why guinea pigs develop ovarian cysts is unknown. Cysts may become very large, up to 4 cm (1.5 inches), and often there is more than one cyst in each ovary. Ovarian cysts have been associated with infertility and symmetric hair loss on the sides and flanks, and some sows gets generally affected with depression and abdominal discomfort. However, it is believed that many sows have cysts without showing any symptoms. Large cysts may be felt through the abdominal wall, while smaller ones can be diagnosed through ultrasonography. If sows have symptoms, surgical therapy is an option (see Ovariohysterectomy).

OVARIOHYSTERECTOMY
A surgical procedure in the sow in which the ovaries and uterus are removed.

This is usually performed because of uterine disease or in conjunction with Caesarean section. Ovarian cysts and removal of mummifications are other possible indications. Ovariohysterectomy is occasionally performed in sows that are kept with a boar and where litters are unwanted. But as it is a smaller, easier and cheaper operation to have the boar castrated, this is often preferred.

OVERGROWN TEETH
See Malocclusion.

'OVERHEATING'
See 'Broken back'.

PARAPHIMOSIS
The boar is unable to retract his penis into the prepuce. The tip of the penis is hanging outside the prepuce. It is often due to foreign bodies, such as seeds or shavings, being trapped in the prepuce folds. These should be gently removed and the prepuce rinsed in sterile saline. If infection occurs, the boar may become infertile. Paraphimosis is commonly seen in castrated boars, but it does not seem to bother them.

PNEUMONIA
An infection in the lungs caused by bacteria, virus or mycoplasms.

Many germs are able to infect guinea pigs and develop pneumonia. Most pigs are resistant against such bacteria; however, some factors may increase susceptibility; these include cold, draughts, ammonia from urine, vitamin C deficiency, pregnancy, overcrowding, stress, and old and young age. The most common bacterium is *Bordetella bronchiseptica*, but many other bacteria, as well as mycoplasms and viruses, may be responsible.

Symptoms are increased respiratory sounds (see Ruttling), a running nose, cough, dyspnoea (laboured respiration), depression and anorexia. Sudden deaths are sometimes seen in pregnant sows. Disease may spread to the middle ear, causing wry neck, or to the uterus, causing abortions. The veterinarian will make the diagnosis by stethoscopy of the lungs and also possibly by radiography and blood tests. If a pig dies, a post-mortem examination is essential for determining the exact cause and to find out which antibiotics are most efficient.

Treatment should be with a broad-spectrum antibiotic and supportive therapy, such as warm, dust- and draught-free surroundings, food correction, improved hygiene, and avoiding stress. It may be possible to get some bovine Bordetella vaccine, which has proved to be quite effective in controlling outbreaks.

PODODERMATITIS
An infection in the foot pad, which causes considerable swelling and pain.

This is a disease more frequently seen in older guinea pigs. Obesity and lack of exercise seem to be predisposing factors, as pododermatitis has some resemblance to bedsores. A heavy guinea pig that sits down a lot does not have an optimal blood circulation due to pressure on the foot pads. This, together with abrasive bedding and poor hygiene, may result in bacterial invasion of the foot pad. Most commonly, a staphylococcal bacteria can be found in such foot abscesses.

Symptoms are a massive swelling of one foot or more. The pig is reluctant to support its weight on the affected foot. Under the foot pad, there is a skin lesion with pus. The lesion is very unlikely to heal. The foot must be cleaned with an antiseptic solution, and an antibiotic treatment (given by injection and/or ointment) may be prescribed by the veterinarian. The cage must be kept very clean, and soft bedding, such as towels, are recommended, as any bandage is likely to fall off.

Complications are quite commonly seen either as an infection spreading to bone tissue (osteomyelitis) or through the bloodstream (see Septicaemia), resulting in death.

POLYDACTYLY
Babies born with extra toes.

Polydactyly is a genetic disorder seen in certain breeds, such as Self-Blacks and Golden Agoutis. It is most commonly seen on the front legs as a single dangling thumb. One or both legs may be affected. Rarely, double extra toes are seen. The hind legs can be affected as well, but this is rare. Most extra toes are nothing more than a tiny nail dangling in a narrow piece of skin but they are likely to cause trouble as they can easily get caught and damaged, so normally they are removed. Polydactyly is a serious fault at shows, and such pigs should not be bred from.

POST-PARTUM SORES
Wounds and hair loss that develops shortly after parturition.

Post-partum sores seem to exist in two distinct forms. The first is situated on the centre back and is thought to be due to nutritional deficiencies. It looks identical to another skin condition, which is often seen in light-coloured and older pigs (see 'Broken back'). The other form is found on the rump and lower abdomen. It is believed that it appears after a prolonged labour, when the sow is too weak and tired to clean herself afterwards. Blood and slime dries out and the skin beneath becomes inflamed. When she wants to clean herself later, it is impossible without pulling out the coat. The skin heals up spontaneously but it may help to use a mild skin antiseptic. If a sow after parturition is observed not to clean herself, the problem should be solved by gently rinsing her with lukewarm water.

PREGNANCY TOXAEMIA
A dreaded disease where pregnant sows become anorectic and apathetic, and die within a few days.

Pregnancy toxaemia is the most dreaded disease in pregnant sows and is seen in the last third of pregnancy or the first few days after birth. In most cases, the mother as well as her babies, is lost. Similar diseases are seen in cats, ponies, cows and sheep and are associated with obesity and a sudden decreased food intake. There may also be some hereditary predisposition, as certain breeds such as Self-Blacks, Golden Agoutis and Satins, seem more susceptible to developing toxaemia.

Pregnancy toxaemia – or just toxaemia – can be divided into two different types: primary or secondary. Primary toxaemia is caused by internal factors. Food intake may be restricted due to a large litter compressing the stomach, making the sow unable to eat enough to meet her and the babies' energy requirements. Another effect of a space occupation in large litters may be that the uterus compresses the large uterine blood vessels compromising the uterine blood supply. Babies will die from suffocation and the uterine wall becomes dark-red, blue or black. The sow becomes depressed and develops toxaemia.

Secondary toxaemia is due to external factors and is by far the commonest type. Stress is a major factor: this may be caused by mobbing, by transportation, by showing or through other diseases. Of the latter, mange and scurvy (see Vitamin C deficiency) are major causes.

In the last trimester of pregnancy, foetuses are fast-growing and need lots of energy and nutrients to develop, especially in the case of a large litter. This means that the sow must eat a lot to meet these demands. If food intake is decreased for whatever primary or secondary reason, she comes into a negative energy balance. To compensate, she starts using her own body reserves – the fat deposits.
Unfortunately, many sows are unable to do this in moderate amounts, instead mobilising far too much fat. That is why obesity plays a big role in the development of toxaemia. There is just so much more fat to be released.

When too much fat instead of sugar is metabolised, dramatic changes happen in the body, changing blood acidity and composition, and making the sow feel unwell and stop eating. Excesses of fat are stored in the liver, making it look pale, and finally liver cells degenerate, causing liver failure. Fat infiltrates the kidneys, causing degeneration as well. This can easily be seen at post-mortem examinations where the liver and kidneys are found yellow and brittle from fatty degeneration. All these changes make the sow more depressed and unwell, creating a vicious circle, which, once entered, is fatal for the sow. Foetuses weaken and die at an early stage, contributing to further aggravation of the condition.

Apart from progressive depression and loss of appetite leading to total anorexia, the sow has a hunched posture and, when handled, feels catatonic and sometimes cold on her ears and feet. If she survives for a couple of days, she will develop a protruding spine and hips, as a consequence of losing body fat and muscle mass.

There is no known treatment for pregnancy toxaemia. All sows are lost. If treatment is attempted, it must include glucose infusions, oral preparations, and glucocorticoid injections. Caesarean section is out of the question because the sow is too sick to survive surgery. Euthanasia is a suitable solution for sows that suffer for too long. Treatment seems to drag out suffering instead of curing it, which must be taken into consideration when choosing between treatment and euthanasia.

As toxaemia is always fatal, every effort must be made to prevent it from developing in the first place. Do not breed from obese sows, only from well-nourished sows in a healthy condition. Avoid stress, such as transportation, showing, food changes and mobbing by cagemates during pregnancy.

PREMATURE BABIES
Babies are born too early to be able to survive but too late for it to be an abortion.

Babies born before the 60th day of gestation are unlikely to survive. They are dead or very weak, small but fully developed. The coat is thin and the claws are soft and white. Most premature litters are due to diseases in the sow. Pregnancy toxaemia, vitamin C deficiency and mange are common causes, but the condition is also seen when two pregnant sows share a hutch (see Birth induction). Sows reject premature, weak babies, and the young are very unlikely to survive if hand-reared.

PRURITUS
The medical term for an itch – a symptom rather than a disease.

Many different skin diseases lead to pruritus. Parasitic infestations are very common causes and should be checked before everything else (see Cheyletiella, Lice, and Mange), but also fungal diseases (see Skin mycoses, and Dermatophytosis) and allergic conditions (see Skin allergy) are possible causes. Some skin diseases have lack of pruritus as important characteristics (see Hormonal alopecia, 'Broken back', and Demodicosis).

Pruritus is initiated by release of inflammatory mediators from white blood cells. Any sort of inflammation may result in pruritus. It may become so severe that the pig scratches and bites itself to draw blood, causing open sores and infected wounds. Symptoms can be efficiently relieved with glucocorticoid injections, but this should never be done unless the original cause is identified and treated.

113

RED EYE
The conjunctiva is red and swollen due to chronic inflammation.
See Conjunctivitis.

RED URINE
The urine is stained red due to a red pigment called porphyrin.
   From time to time, guinea pig urine contains a red pigment called porphyrin. Sometimes, it is associated with eating food rich in vitamin A (e.g. dandelions). Sometimes, there is no obvious cause. The condition is not associated with disease. Urinalysis shows no red blood cells in urine and the pig has normal urination. Red urine should not be mistaken for infection in the bladder (see Cystitis) or stone formation in the bladder (see Urinary calculi).

REJECTION OF BABIES
The sow refuses to nurse and suckle her babies.
   While most sows are, instinctively, good and caring mothers, some sows reject their newborn babies. Normal babies will follow their mum and find their way to her nipples, and they will make a lot of noise and movement when she cleans them after birth and feeding. This stimulates her maternal feelings. If, however, babies are quiet, weak, and unable to follow her around the hutch (see Premature babies, and Weak babies), there will be no stimulation of her maternal instincts and she will abandon them.
   It is not unusual to see inexperienced mothers panic when having their first litter. Every time a baby approaches her, she will run away and hide in the farthest corner. Such a sow is best placed with her babies in a small, dark box in a quiet place. She will then be unable to escape, and, after a few hours, she will accept her babies. On very rare occasions, it may be necessary to give the sow a mild sedative injection. In most cases, she will be the perfect mother next time she has a litter.
   However, there are lines where poor maternal instincts are quite common. Such sows will reject their next litter as well. As this is probably hereditary, these lines should be excluded from breeding.
   Rejection may also be due to the sow being exhausted after a difficult labour or because she suffers from an infection (see Mastitis, and Metritis) or from a metabolic disease (see Pregnancy toxaemia). In cases of the continuous rejection of well-developed babies, they must be hand-reared (see Orphan babies).

RESORPTION
An early miscarriage without vaginal discharge.
Foetal resorption during the first trimester of gestation is quite common in the guinea pig and is usually unnoticed by the owner. If the sow is in with a boar, it may just seem as though she needs some extra time to become pregnant. The commonest cause is an error in the development in the foetus or foetal membranes, but malnutrition and mange are other common triggers. When the litter is dead, all uterine contents are dissolved and absorbed by the uterus, and complications such as uterine infections are rare. The sow usually comes into oestrus quite soon and fertility is not affected.

RINGWORM
See Dermatophytosis.

RUNNING LICE
See Lice.

RUTTLING
A dissonance from the nose or upper airways caused by mucosal swelling.
This is a peculiar sound, heard simultaneously with inspiration, and is caused by a swelling or an excess of mucosal membranes in the airways. Most pigs are unaffected. Ruttling is a serious show fault. One type of ruttling is heard in very short-nosed pigs where mucosal folds are believed to vibrate in the air flow in a similar way to that which happens in Bulldogs.
Such pigs should not be shown or bred from. A more common type is caused by mucosal swelling restricting the air flow. Swelling can be caused by a mild infection or by dust irritation or allergy. If the pig is unaffected, no treatment is necessary, but, in cases of infection, a short antibiotic treatment may be useful. The pig must be kept in as dust-free surroundings as possible. Sometimes, ruttling can be aggravated and difficulty in breathing occurs. This may be due to complications in the lower airways (see Inhalant allergy).

SCOURS
See Diarrhoea.

SCURVY
See Vitamin C deficiency.

SEBORRHOEA
A skin condition characterised by dandruff, scabs and a greasy coat.

Seborrhoea is not a disease but a symptom signifying that the skin is irritated. In this case, skin reacts by speeding up multiplication reducing the time from when a skin cell is produced till it becomes shed from the surface. Grease glands overreact as well. This means a build-up of grease and flakes of dead skin (dandruff) on the surface. Greasy coat often causes pruritus (itching), and grease is a great growth medium for bacteria and yeasts, so secondary infections are not uncommon.

Many different conditions may lead to seborrhoea. Inflammation from external parasites and ringworm are classic causes, but also allergic conditions, mycoses, bacterial infections and liver disease are common causes. Treatment of seborrhoea is dependent upon diagnosing the cause and eliminating it. However, seborrhoea may be alleviated by using a suitable medical shampoo, as often as necessary. Such shampoos not only remove grease and skin debris, but some of the ingredients also delay skin multiplication, thus normalising the condition.

SELLNICK
See Mange.

SEPTICAEMIA
Spreading of an infection from its primary site through the bloodstream to other parts of the body (blood poisoning).

Bacteria, or viruses leading to septicaemia, may invade the bloodstream from any infectious site: a bite wound, a foot abscess, uterine infection, cystitis, etc. Bacteria circulating in the blood can colonise any organ, e.g. the joints, the liver and the spleen. Not surprisingly, the pig is severely depressed, often with high fever, and death is the rule more than the exception. Only if a bacterium is identified and treated very quickly is there hope. If there are more pigs in the household, it is a very good idea to have any pigs dying from an unknown cause examined post-mortem to identify the cause of death, in case other pigs become ill.

SKIN ALLERGY
A condition in which the skin becomes hypersensitive to itself or to things in the surrounding environment, causing skin symptoms (see Seborrhoea) and itching (see Pruritus).

Skin infections are common as a result of biting and scratching. When developing a skin allergy, some immune-defence mechanisms that were meant to protect the pig against intruding micro-organisms are suddenly sensitised against harmless matters. It could be a contact allergy against substances that come into contact with the skin (e.g. printing ink from newspaper bedding, perfume from shampoos, ingredients in antiparasitic sprays, etc.). Mites and insects are very allergenic (allergy inducing), especially if they sting, bite or burrow in the skin, because their saliva is composed of many irritating compounds. But the surface of the parasite may also act as an allergen and often the allergic response is far more serious than the presence of the parasite. A very serious allergic skin disease is one in which the immune system regards skin cells as intruders, thus trying to isolate them from its own skin. Such disorders are called autoimmune diseases.

When treating allergies, it is of utmost importance to identify the allergen, as its removal will resolve symptoms. But this is easier said than done, as there are no reliable tests in guinea pigs, to demonstrate what the pig reacts against. Elimination trials may be useful. Glucocorticoid preparations are also effective, but should be used with extreme care, as they have many side effects. Severely affected guinea pigs are better euthanased.

SKIN MYCOSES
Mycotic infections in the skin, apart from ringworm (see Dermatophytosis), causing varying signs.
Some breeds (Rex and Satins) are more susceptible to skin mycoses. Symptoms vary from a greasy coat with mild hair loss (see Seborrhoea) to severe skin changes with scabs and sores.

It may look exactly like mite infestation (see Mange), and, if treatment with avermectins fail, skin mycosis should be considered. The condition may or may not be pruritic (itchy) but is not contagious. Sometimes, skin symptoms are complicated by the organism spreading into the oral cavity, the lungs and the kidneys (see Candidiasis).

Diagnosis is based upon identification of the causal micro-organism, although it may prove difficult. However, any seborrhoeic skin

condition that does not respond after a mange treatment should be treated like a mycosis, with repeated washes in antimycotic shampoos as prescribed by the veterinarian.

117

SNUFFLES
See Ruttling.

SORE NIPPLES
Damage to the nipples caused by suckling babies.
   This can be seen when rearing large litters or when milk production is scarce (see Agalactia). This means that babies will pull and bite the nipples, making them red, swollen and sore. In this case, mammary gland infection is a common complication (see Mastitis). In uncomplicated cases, the application of a camomile ointment is sufficient. Feeding with juicy greens will increase milk production.

SPINAL CORD INJURY
See Hind limb paralysis.

STATIC LICE
See Hay mites.

STILLBORN BABIES
Babies are dead when born or die immediately after birth.
   It is not uncommon for a sow to deliver one or more dead babies. Many babies die within their foetal membranes because the mother does not unwrap them. If the baby is big and strong, it may break out from the membranes by its own force, but weaker babies may fail to do so. Deaths from unwrapping are often seen in large litters where babies are arriving within short intervals and with inexperienced mothers. If babies are born with their rear legs first, the sow may simply clean the wrong end of the baby, leaving the head inside the membranes. Stillborn babies can also be seen after prolonged and difficult parturitions (see Dystocia), where the babies suffocate inside the pelvic canal. This is particularly the case if the baby is large or if the pelvic canal is rigid. Some babies die before parturition, because the sow is ill (see Vitamin C deficiency, and Pregnancy Toxaemia).

STROKE
See Sudden death.

SUDDEN DEATH
The guinea pig is found dead without any previous signs of disease.
   Although death is often experienced as sudden in guinea pigs, it may

not be so. As a hunted animal, they seem to mask any disease symptom until very late and death may occur before the owner has noticed any symptoms. Possible causes for sudden death are heart attack, infection (see Enteritis, Pneumonia, and Septicaemia), reproductive disorders (see Pregnancy toxaemia, Dystocia, and Uterine Haemorrhage), gastrointestinal emergencies (see Gastric dilation and torsion, and Bloat), overheating (see Heat stroke) and several others. If sudden death occurs in a colony of pigs, the cause of death should be determined, in case a contagious disease is involved.

SUN BURN
Hairless areas, such as the ears, become swollen, sore and red.

If a guinea pig is left outside in a run with no shade, it may become sun burned. White pigs in particular are susceptible. Sunburned ears can be treated by being bathed in cold water and with applications of a local analgesic (e.g. lidocaine) to the ears. Sun block for children may be used for sunburn protection.

TOOTH ABSCESS
See Abscesses, and Malocclusion.

TOXAEMIA
See Pregnancy toxaemia.

UROLITHIASIS
The formation of stones in the urinary system, mainly in the bladder or urethra.

Guinea pig urine is creamy and opaque. The opacity is due to the excretion of calcium crystals, mainly calcium carbonate and calcium dihydrate. As guinea pigs excrete calcium excess through the kidneys, stone formation may occur. In sows, these are often passed through the urethra, but they are unable to exit the small urinary orifice. The stone can easily be felt and minor stones can be pressed out between two fingers. Larger stones can be removed after a small scalpel incision, made on a sedated pig.

In boars, the problem is bigger because of their long and narrow urethra. A common place for stones to fasten is where the urethra passes the penis bone, and it may be difficult or impossible to remove them. Older boars often get obstructed by a combination of coagulated secretions from the bulbourethral glands and calcium crystals. In any case, the veterinarian must be consulted.

119

In both sows and boars, a stone may block the urinary passage partly or completely. In the first case, urination is possible but delayed, often combined with straining. In the second case, a life-threatening and extremely painful condition occurs. The bladder becomes distended and the kidneys stop functioning, leading to a build-up of toxic waste products in the blood. Without treatment, death will occur in one to two days. Calculi in the bladder do not produce such alarming symptoms, but lead to hematuria (bloody urine) and infection (see Cystitis). Calculi should be suspected if cystitis recurs after antibiotic treatment. Diagnosis can be made by clinical signs followed by radiography. Calculi should be removed manually or by surgery. After removal the pig must be fed on a restricted calcium diet (e.g. no alfalfa, clover or dandelion leaves). Acidification of the urine may dissolve smaller calculi. High doses of vitamin C (100 mg per day) may prove helpful.

UTERINE HAEMORRHAGE
Bleeding from the uterus can be seen as a bloody vaginal discharge.
Uterine haemorrhage is a symptom that can have many causes. If the sow is pregnant, it is usually the first sign of an abortion. Bleeding may fill the pregnant uterine horns and the sow will deteriorate rapidly. Many sows will die even if ovariohysterectomy is attempted. Bleeding immediately after birth may be due to trauma or vitamin K deficiency. An injection to contract the uterus, plus one with vitamin K, may cause the bleeding to stop.

Non-pregnant sows may develop uterine infections or cystic metritis (see Metritis). Surgical intervention (see Ovariohysterectomy) is the most efficient cure. Vaginal discharge should not be confused with blood or red pigment in the urine.

UTERINE PROLAPSE
The uterus is expelled through the vagina at, or shortly after, parturition.
The prolapse may be due to trauma during difficulty in parturition (see Dystocia) or seen in older, malnourished sows. It also occurs when two pregnant sows share a hutch and one of them litters (see Birth induction). It is a very serious condition and quick action is needed to save the sow. Chances are better if the prolapse is new and minor, the uterus is pink to dark red and the sow is still relatively unaffected. However, if the prolapse is older, very large, the uterus is bluish-black with gangrene and the sow is severely affected, her

chances are very poor and euthanasia should be performed. Treatment (for unaffected sows only) involves an oxytocin injection, but, if unsuccessful, surgery (see Ovariohysterectomy) or closure of the vaginal opening may be tried.

VITAMIN C DEFICIENCY

Guinea pigs need a daily supplement of vitamin C (ascorbic acid). Deficiency leads to retarded growth, dental and breeding problems and a deficient immune system.

Guinea pigs, like humans and other primates, are unable to produce an enzyme essential for vitamin C synthesis. This means that vitamin C must be supplied from the food. Moreover, vitamin C is not stored in the organism and an excess of the vitamin is excreted through the urine. Thus supplementation must be done on a daily basis. Adult guinea pigs need 10 mg vitamin C per kg (2 lbs) of body weight. Growing youngsters and pregnant and suckling sows need up to 30 mg per day.

Vitamin C is essential in bone and connective tissue formation. Growth of good, strong bones and healthy joints, as well as the development of good-quality, well-positioned teeth, is dependent on vitamin C. Blood vessels owe their strength to the formation of healthy connective tissue. Vitamin C is also important for an efficient immune system, and it is a part of the production of various hormones.

Deficiency occurs when vitamin C is supplied in insufficient amounts. This happens mainly during the winter when grass and outdoor greens are difficult to find. Many fruits and vegetables fed are low in vitamin C, especially in late winter where storage has deteriorated the vitamin C content. Carrots, beetroot, apples and sugar beets are too low in vitamin C for pregnant, suckling and growing pigs. Most dry foods do not contain vitamin C, and supplementation of the vitamin in drinking water is unreliable, as it quickly degrades in the air and light.

Mild vitamin C deficiency causes only small and unspecific symptoms. Pigs do not seem as vigorous, the average lifespan is shorter, youngsters do not grow as well, and there is a small increase in abortions, pregnancy toxaemia and stillborn or weak youngsters.

In cases of more severe deficiency, a disease called scurvy develops. Growth in youngsters stops, sometimes permanently. Joint swellings are seen, particularly in the hocks and knees, due to bleeding in the joint. Weakening of connective tissue in the blood vessels may also cause intestinal and mucous membrane bleeding. Pigs develop a stiff hip, which makes them unable to move their hind legs separately. Instead, they jump around with both hind legs at the same time – like a rabbit (so-called 'hoppers'). Some pigs may even develop hind leg paralysis. The guinea pig becomes hunched and meagre. Breeding does not succeed at all. There are all sorts of problems: infertility, resorptions and abortions, pregnancy toxaemia, uterine bleedings or infections, stillborn and weak babies. Guinea pigs with scurvy are very susceptible to infections, and otherwise harmless germs may cause a fatal infection. Sometimes, epidemics of diarrhoea or pneumonia break out in a colony of guinea pigs suffering from scurvy, causing big losses.

When diagnosed, vitamin C deficiency must be corrected by adding a supplement to the food. Cavy pellets with added vitamin C are suitable. Vegetables with a high vitamin C content should be fed. These include kale and cabbage, broccoli, swedes and parsley. In cases of scurvy, extra vitamin C must be given for a minimum of 10 days or until signs (e.g. bleeding, hind leg paralysis or 'hopping') resolve. Human ascorbic acid tablets may be used at a daily dose of 100 mg per kg (2 lbs) of body weight. They can be crushed and dissolved in a little water and given through the mouth. Most pigs will recover completely, but some seem to suffer permanent damage. Breeders in particular must ensure that vitamin C deficiency never occurs, by feeding dry food for guinea pigs, selecting vegetables with a high vitamin C content in the winter, and plenty of grass and other outdoor greens in the summer.

VITAMIN D TOXICITY

An oversupplementation of vitamin D leads to weak bones (osteoporosis) and calcifications in soft organs.

Many guinea pig owners oversupplement their guinea pigs with cod liver oil, which is rich in vitamin D, because they believe it increases coat lustre. However, vitamin D is never a problem when feeding a diet containing sun-dried hay, carrots, grass and dry food. Vitamin D toxicity has also been described due to feeding certain brands of rabbit pellets, where vitamin D contents are much higher than the maximum of 1500 i.u. per kg (2 lbs) of food, which is recommended for guinea pigs. Too much vitamin D leads to the removal of calcium from the bones, causing hind leg paralysis and bone weakness. The excess of calcium in the bloodstream leads to depositions of calcium in the soft organs, such as muscles, lungs, stomach and intestines. This causes unspecific symptoms, including weakening, weight loss and death. Diagnosis is made by symptoms or at post mortem. Treatment is withdrawal of the Vitamin D source and supportive therapy until the signs resolve.

WALKING DANDRUFF
See Cheyletiella.

WASTING DISEASE
A disease in which the guinea pig drinks far too much and loses weight.

Wasting disease is mainly seen in older pigs, four years or above. Water consumption increases dramatically and the pig is able to empty several water bottles every day. It urinates just as much as it drinks. At the same time, it loses weight despite having a good appetite. Even when it becomes very thin, it still is happy and active. At the end stage of the disease, the pig may look unwell for a few hours before it dies. Death is often preceded by a drop in water intake. The disease may go on for a few months, but many pigs have survived for more than a year.

It is believed that there are two different causes for wasting disease. The first is that high sugar levels in urine drag water into the urine (see Diabetes). The second is that the kidneys become unable to concentrate urine, leading to excessive urination (see Kidney failure). In both cases, loss of water through the urine is responsible for increased thirst.

WEAK BABIES
Babies are born alive but die within a few days because they are unable to suckle and follow the sow.

Weak-born babies are often smallish. It is very common in large litters of five or more babies where one or two babies are smaller and weaker than the rest of the litter, probably because they were positioned in less favourable parts of the uterus where the blood supply was suboptimal. Such babies are usually unable to fight against their littermates for the nipples, of which there are only two. If babies are born before term, they are small and unable to survive (see Premature babies, and Induced birth). If parturition has been difficult, the babies may have been damaged, i.e. oxygen deficiency causes brain damage, which causes weakness in the newborn. Weakness may also occur in the uterus if the sow suffers from disease (see Vitamin C deficiency, and Pregnancy toxaemia).

ZOONOSES
These are diseases that can be transmitted from animals to humans.

There are only a few diseases that can be transmitted from guinea pigs to humans. The most serious are salmonella and yersinia bacteria, which cause scours and intestinal infections (see Diarrhoea, and Enteritis). This should be borne in mind in case of outbreaks in guinea pig colonies, and culling may be necessary because of the human health hazard. Ringworm (see Dermatophytosis) causes skin disease in many mammals. Children and young animals are most frequently affected. If a child develops ringworm, animals in contact should be tested.

SECTION III:
VARIETIES, BREEDING & SHOWING

CHAPTER 9

GUINEA PIG VARIETIES

1. Coat type
2. Purebreed cavies
3. The self cavy
4. Non-self varieties
5. Rarer varieties

There is no such thing as the perfect guinea pig and, for most guinea pig fanciers, their favourite is the one they happen to have in their hands at any particular moment. But guinea pigs do come in many varieties and this chapter will give you a guide to the type that will best suit you. Do you want a pet, do you want to show your guinea pig or do you want a slightly exotic variety – bearing in mind that it will require more care?

1. COAT TYPE

Cavies have hair, not fur, and, as with humans, it can be straight, curly or frizzy. Some cavies have smooth hair, some rough hair, some long hair. For ease of definition we will firstly divide them into the length of hair and then later look at the specific breeds.

SMOOTH-HAIRED CAVIES

These cavies have smooth hair and the coat lies in the direction of head to tail stump with no waves or rosettes at all. The coat is made of two layers of hair. The guard hairs, as they are called, are strong, coarse hair forming the top layer of the coat and there is a short layer of much softer hair under. When the guard hairs have been groomed out, this under layer is much softer and shinier than the guard hairs and gives the smooth-haired cavy a velvety sheen.

Many colours are available in smooth-haired cavies, ranging from one colour to several colours that can be random patches or in recognised patterns.

Some breeds also have hairs that have one colour for the main shaft of the hair and a second colour on the tip; this second colour often has a metallic tone, which gives these cavies a different appearance to the other smooth-haired breeds.

When showing cavies, a considerable time needs to be spent over about two weeks preparing them. It is much better to spend five to ten minutes a day during this time of preparation, rather than leaving it all to the last day, as this is far more stressful to the cavy and to the exhibitor.

LONG-HAIRED CAVIES

There are currently six long-haired breeds recognised. Of these, three have smooth hair, which lies in various stipulated ways. The other three have developed from crosses between these breeds and another breed with a curly coat, the Merino, which will be discussed later.

The hair on all these long-haired breeds grows at the rate of approximately one inch a month and, for this reason, most of them quite often require the hair to be trimmed to keep the coat from getting tangled in the hay and matted up. If the hair gets matted, it must be cut out carefully.

When these breeds are being shown as purebreed cavies they have to have their hair brushed and combed daily and kept in 'wrappers' or special curlers, as they must have their hair kept to the full length and not allowed to curl at the ends.

SPECIAL COATS

There are three main breeds of cavy that have different types of coat to those mentioned above.

One is the Crested Cavy, which has a predominately smooth coat but has a crest or rosette of hair on its head just between its eyes. The crest can either be of the same coloured hair as the body of the cavy or can be of a contrasting colour. Some of the other breeds of smooth cavy have been bred to have a crest as well as the main attributes of the dominant breed

We then come to the Abyssinian cavy. This breed has a number of rosettes and ridges in the coat. These are in a certain order over the sides and rump of the animal so that there is a recognised pattern, with the rosettes giving rise to ridges of hair between the rosettes.

Also in this group of cavies with different coat types are the Rex cavies. These have a thick, curly or almost frizzy undercoat with longer guard hairs. The coat on Rex cavies runs from rump to head and stands out, giving the appearance of a very tubby animal!

2. PUREBREED CAVIES

Purebreed cavies are shown under three 'Standards'. The majority of purebreed cavies fall into the classification of 'Full Standard'. These cavies are bred by fanciers who are interested in trying to breed cavies to a defined standard. The British Cavy Council, working with the individual breed clubs interested in the breed concerned, lays down these standards.

There is also a Guide Standard Classification, which applies to cavies of a breed that has shown it has potentially reached the stage where standards can be agreed on but there are still some developmental details to be settled.

The third classification is Unstandardised. This normally applies to new breeds of cavy, which have been bred, usually by a small number of fanciers.

They are not allowed to be entered in shows as purebreeds, due to the fact that the breed has not yet become established, it has not yet been possible to assess the breed, which means that the definitions of the breed have not yet been decided upon. Although the ideal conformation of the cavy is the same for all cavies, it does not carry the same importance in all breeds, as the various coat types can take precedence over the shape of the animal.

THE SHOW ANIMAL

Shape: The ideal shape for a cavy should be compact with a broad nose with plenty of width between its eyes, which should be big, bright and bold.

Ears: The ears should be large, petal shaped and set fairly low on the side of the head. They should drop slightly. Ideally the profile should be somewhat 'Roman' not snipey.

Body: The Cavy should have a good shoulder and then slope gently to the rump.

General aspect: All animals must be healthy and well looked after in order to be judged fit to show and possibly win a class.

3. THE SELF-CAVY

This cavy is a smooth-haired cavy and, for showing purposes, must have only one colour hair. There are 12 recognised colours of Self-Cavy. There are also a small number of colours that are still in the stage of proving themselves to be of the standard required as to consistency of breeding true to the defined colour.

Another aspect of gaining recognition for a new colour is that there have to be a reasonable number of breeders interested in developing and showing that particular colour. This stipulation is there because it will ensure that there is a definite pool of breeding stock available, that other interested people may find it possible to obtain breeding stock before the cavy is given a 'Full Standard'.

We will now take a view of each colour individually.

THE PINK EYED WHITE

This cavy is fully described by its name. It is a large cavy with a pure white coat. The eyes should be large and pink in colour. It is not an albino, although this is how it is often described by newcomers and the general public. The ears should be like a large rose petal and should be pink, as should the pads of the feet. The toenails must be white. It is about the only breed of cavy that carries no other colour. This cavy can be difficult to show to perfection, as it is imperative that it is perfectly clean and that it has not stained its tummy. As you can imagine, this can be a problem as it lies in its cage.

Pink Eyed White cavies, which are being used as show stock, are not usually fed carrots, especially near show time, as it can stain the hair around the mouth. The coat of these cavies can be smooth and easy to groom, but I have found that some animals with the best conformation have a very thick and sometimes longer-than-average coat. Woolly-coated pigs never make an exhibition pig and should not be bred from. Another serious fault is a very thin, cottony coat. Whites are also bred with dark eyes and these will be described later.

THE SELF-BLACK

This is a very popular breed, with its raven-black glossy coat showing very well after grooming. Probably more blacks than any other colour are bred to the conformation aimed for. This is especially true of the boars, which often excel in shoulder definition, while the sows often have a very good profile.

However, the best blacks often carry red and/or white hairs, which spoil their appearance. A judge will fault such a pig, quite correctly, on colour. They have an advantage over white and other paler cavies in that they do not show stains as much.

One problem with black cavies is that often, although the top coat is a beautiful deep black, the colour does not reach to the bottom of the shaft of the hair and the under colour of the coat looks a dull, greyish black. Unfortunately, the animals with the best under colour are often those carrying most red hairs. These do not make show animals and should be used for breeding pruposes only. The eyes, ears, pads and nails of Self-Black cavies must all be black. Poor depth of colour in Blacks is mostly caused by white hairs in the breeding stock. Red improves the colour.

THE SELF-CREAM

The ideal shade for a Self-Cream cavy is often described as that of 'Devon Cream', and it is a difficult colour to aim for. It is another breed that has a problem with under colour pigmentation. The animals where the cream colouring is carried down to the skin are almost always too dark on the surface, while those of the correct top colour seem to fade to almost white under and must be faulted by the judge.

As with the Self-Whites, the cream cavy is a large breed with plenty of width between the eyes. The eyes of a cream cavy should be ruby while the ears and pads should be pink. When grooming the creams you have to be careful not to remove too many of the hairs to leave a patchy appearance.

Self-Creams are also prone to staining around the rear-end in the same way as the Self-Whites. A patchy appearance is a bad fault, rendering such a pig unsuitable for showing.

THE PINK EYED GOLDEN

This is another of the self-cavies that has two slightly different colour options. The Pink Eyed Golden is also a very popular breed. The coat should be of a medium golden colour, neither looking 'brassy' nor having a red tint.

Again, the under colour is a problem and, if the grooming is not done carefully, they can look patchy or flaky. This especially happens on the sides of the animal, which detracts from the appearance and, as with the blacks, golden cavies can often have coarse white hairs. Breeding stock should be a good colour to the skin, otherwise the depth of colour gets worse in the breeding and will be faulted by the judge. It is another breed that has good conformation and is often one of the largest breeds. Goldens are also bred with dark eyes.

These first four breeds are probably the most popular of the Selfs at shows and regularly win the Best Self and Best In Show accolades. However, they are not the only Self colours.

THE SELF-RED

This cavy is not as popular now as it used to be. The colour should be a mahogany red. Unfortunately, the head of a Self-Red is often narrower than is desired, which gives the animal a snipey profile that does not look as attractive. The ears should have a dark red/brown colour and the feet and eyes should also be dark.

THE SELF-CHOCOLATE

This cavy should be the colour of a good dark chocolate bar and have dark ruby eyes. Unfortunately, as with so many of the dark colour types, lighter creamy hairs will appear, particularly on the face, body and around the vent. Use sound colour for breeding stock.

THE SELF-BEIGE

Think of the colour of beige material. Possibly crème caramel is a better comparison. The eyes are pink. There can be varying shades in animals from the same litter. One bonus of the colour is that what you see on the top goes right down to the skin. When breeding for this colour, use a dark sow or boar with its opposite colour – dark with light, light with dark.

THE SELF-LILAC

The colour should be dark lilac to dove grey, and tends to fade as the animal matures. Again, when breeding for this colour, use light with dark, not two lights or two darks together. This cavy should also have pink eyes.

THE BUFF AND THE SAFFRON

Some people believe that the Buffs are just dark creams. However, Buffs bred to Buffs breed true, and do not produce creams. They should be a deep rich Buff shade, with no hint of lemon, apricot or cream. They are dark-eyed.

The Saffron, which looks similar, should, however, have pink eyes and the coat should be a medium sand colour.

Here is the standard of excellence of the English Self Cavy Club based on **100 points** divided as follows:

Colour For All English Self Cavies:
Top colour: lustrous and of even shade all over the head and body.
Undercolour: to match top colour down to the skin, giving an
appearance free from flakiness. Hair on feet to match body colour. **30**

Type: broad Roman nose with a good width of muzzle, rounded at the
nostrils, short and cobby body with very deep, broad, shoulders. **25**
Coat: short and silky with glossy sheen **15**
Ears: rose petal shape, set wide apart, large and drooping **10**
Eyes: large and bold **10**
Presentation: condition, cleanliness and grooming **10**

Together with the standard, detailed remarks are given for each colour
as follows:
Whites: pure snow white. Eyes pink or black. Ears pink/white. Pads
flesh pink.
Blacks: colour deep and lustrous. Eyes, ears and pads black.
Creams: pale, even colour, free from lemon or yellow tinge. Eyes ruby.
Ears pink/cream. Pads flesh pink.
Goldens: medium colour with no suggestion of yellow, brassiness or
redness. Eyes pink or dark. Ears and pads pink/golden.
Reds: dark, rich colour. Eyes dark ruby. Ears and pads dark red/brown.
Chocolates: rich, dark colour. Eyes ruby. Ears and pads chocolate.
Beige: even, medium colour. Eyes pink. Ears and pads pink/beige.
Lilac: even, medium dove-grey colour, no suggestion of beige. Eyes
pink. Ears and pads pink/lilac.
Saffron: medium sand colour. Eyes pink. Ears and pads pink.
Buff: a deep rich buff shade with no hint of lemon, apricot or cream.
Eyes dark. Ears pink/buff. Pads flesh pink.

4. THE NON-SELF VARIETIES

These cavies may be smooth-haired in various colours, or
they can be long-haired, or have rosettes in their coats.

THE ABYSSINIAN
This is one of the most striking of guinea pigs, with rosettes in its coat
and shades of colour. For showing purposes, it requires less
preparation than a lot of other varieties, but to produce an Abyssinian
that conforms to the show standard needs a lot of thought. The
requirements are specific.
   Although the Abyssinian, or Abby as it is known to its devotees, has

a rough coat, the formation of the rosettes is of utmost importance. Each rosette should be deep, emanating from a pin-point centre. There should be four of them in a straight line of the saddle of the body, four around the rump and one or two on each shoulder. Then there are the ridges: these are formed when one rosette meets another. The ridges thus formed should run in straight lines, across the body and down the sides. Any sign of a flat coat anywhere on the animal is not good. An Abby should also have what looks like a little moustache.

If you are thinking of showing your Abyssinian, look carefully at it. If the rosettes looked double centred, the ridges are uneven or the coat is soft or long, do not show it. Colour is important when showing any variety; coats of a single colour tend to be too soft. Roans, Brindles, and Tortoiseshells and White tend to have better textured coats.

> **Top tip:** *Groom your Abby with a small-bristled brush. Never give a bath before a show as the coat will become soft, not harsh as required.*

The Standard for the Abyssinian gives **100 points** as follows:

Rosettes	**20**
Ridges	**20**
Coat	**20**
Shape and size	**10**
Head furnishings and mane	**15**
Colour	**5**
Eyes and ears	**5**
Condition	**5**

THE AGOUTI

Many people believe that the agouti coat is one of the most attractive that any animal – of whatever breed where this type is presented – can have. Each individual coat hair contains two distinct shades. On a smooth coat, these create a banded effect, which is particularly startling when sunlight falls upon it. Agouti coats tend to have a little sparkle about them. The most common colours are golden and silver. Silver and lemon agoutis have dark eyes; chocolate, cinnamon and cream agoutis have ruby eyes.

DESCRIPTION OF COLOURS

Golden: Deep black undercolour with dark golden ticking. Belly to be an even, rich mahogany and free from brassiness. Ears and pads black; eyes dark.

Silver: deep black undercolour with silver ticking. Belly to be a rich, even, silver and free from whiteness. Ears and pads black; eyes dark.
Cinnamon: deep, rich, cinnamon undercolour with silver ticking. Belly to be rich, even, cinnamon. Ears and pads cinnamon; eyes ruby.
Lemon: deep black undercolour with lemon ticking. Belly colour to be even lemon. ears and pads black; eyes dark.
Chocolate: rich, deep chocolate undercolour with orange ticking. Belly colour to be rich, even, orange. Ears and pads chocolate; eyes ruby.
Cream: rich, deep, chocolate undercolour with lemon ticking. Belly colour to be even lemon. Ears and pads chocolate; eyes ruby.

If your Agouti has long, coarse guard hairs, which spoil the appearance of the ticking, eye circles of a lighter colour than the rest of the coat, or any patches of coat that do not fit in with the general pattern, then it is not suitable for showing.

The Standard for Agouti, scoring out of **100**, is:

Colour	**20**
Ticking	**30**
Shape	**20**
Eyes – large and bold	**5**
Ears – well shaped and drooped	**5**
Size	**5**
Coat and condition	**15**

THE ARGENTE
This is a variation on the Agouti. It has pink eyes but it has ticking on its coat. The most commonly accepted colour is a lilac-based coat with gold ticking. It has been seen in several colours.
Golden/Lilac: dark/deep lilac undercolour with golden ticking. Belly colour to be the same as the ticking colour. Ears and pads to be pink.
Golden/Beige: dark/deep beige undercolour with golden ticking. Belly colour to be the same as the ticking colour. Ears and pads to be pink.
White/Lilac: dark/deep lilac undercolour with white ticking. Belly colour to be the same as the ticking colour. Ears and pads to be pink.
White/Beige: dark/deep beige undercolour with white ticking. Belly colour to be the same as the ticking colour. Ears and pads to be pink.
Lemon/Lilac: dark/deep lilac undercolour with lemon ticking. Belly colour to be the same as the ticking colour. Ears and pads to be pink.
Lemon/Beige: dark/deep beige undercolour with lemonticking. Belly colour to be the same as the ticking colour. Ears and pads to be pink.

BI-COLOURS
These pigs have patches of two colours (other than black and red) and may include Agouti.

BRINDLES
This is an old variety of guinea pig, and one that is very difficult to breed. The coat should consist of an even intermingling of black and red hairs.

THE CRESTED GUINEA PIG
This variety originated in the US and was imported into the UK in 1972. Its name derives from the rosette, which is centrally placed on the forehead, above the eyes but below the ears. The hairs radiate from the crest's central hair point.

The rest of the animal's coat is smooth. The English Crested is self-coloured with the crest of the same colour. In the American Crested the rosette is of a contrasting colour. Probably the most popular of these are the Golden and the Black.

The Standard for the English Crested has **100 points** made up as follows:

Crest – matching body colour   20
Colour – conforms to colours of the matching British English Self 24
Shape – short, cobby; deep, broad shoulders   20
Coat – short and silky   12
Ears – rose petal shaped, set wide apart, slightly drooping   8
Eyes – large and bold   8
Condition   8

THE CORONET
The all-important coronet on this pig should be neat and symmetrical, adorning the head to give a balanced appearance. The coronet should radiate from a small central point. For more detailed information, check the most recent Breed Standard.

THE DUTCH
This is a balanced marked exhibit, which is very hard to breed. It has round cheek markings that should not take in the smellers (whiskers), but should be as near as possible without touching. The blaze should be wedge-shaped, broadest at the base and tapering to a point between the ears. The area behind the ears should be free of coloured hairs.

The saddle divides the body in two. The front is white and the rear is coloured, with the saddle being the dividing line between the two.

The undercut on the belly-line of the saddle should be straight and clear. The stops (white markings on the hind feet) ideally should finish halfway between the toe ends and the hock (heel). There must be one on each hind foot. The ears should be a solid colour.

The Dutch comes in nine different colours. They can be exhibited with faults and penalised accordingly.

The Breed Standard's **100 points** for the Dutch are distributed as follows:

Blaze and cheeks	**15**
Clean neck	**10**
Saddle	**10**
Undercut	**10**
Feet stops	**15**
Ears	**15**
Eyes	**5**
Colour	**10**
Size, shape, coat and condition	**10**

THE HIMALAYAN

This is a pointed pig, which means that it has a white body with darker highlights, ideally either black or chocolate, on the ears, nose and feet.

Himalayans are born white, and the dark points begin to show at a few weeks of age. It takes months for the correct density of the points to develop. The points appear on the nose (the smut as it is called), which should be large, with the colour extending to between the eyes as well as into the whiskers. The ears should be of a matching colour and so should the feet, but the colour must not extend as far as the hocks.

The colour on the points will fade if knocked; bright light also makes the points fade. These pigs should be housed in hutches out of direct sunlight. Unfortunately, the colour can change with the temperature in which the guinea lives. In hot weather, the points can fade. The points often do not appear until the animal is over six months old and also fade with age.

If your Himalayan has white toes or toenails, white patches on its feet or ears, or flesh-coloured ears, then it would be disqualified. Such a Himalayan is not suitable as breeding stock.

THE PERUVIAN

Long-haired cavies are astonishing animals to see – but they also need more care. This is particularly true of the Peruvian. This pig is not for the faint-hearted or the beginner. Its hair has to be brushed every day.

Basically, it is the long-haired version of the Abyssinian. It has rosettes, but these make the hair on the top of the body fall over the face, and the hair at the other end fall over the hindquarters. And this is hair that can grow up to 50 cms (20 inches) in length. Sometimes it is difficult to determine which end of the pig you are looking at.

At birth, Peruvians are short-coated, with two rosettes. One of these grows forwards, the other backwards. The hair below the rosettes grows downwards. As the animal develops, the top hair parts and spills downwards. If the guinea pig is being kept purely as a pet, then the coat needs to be clipped, bathed and brushed, otherwise problems can occur. Without constant care, the coat becomes matted.

For show purposes, the hair is put in wrappers (see page 173). If your Peruvian really objects to this treatment, do not show it.

The Standard for the Peruvian has **100 points** divided so:

Head – broad, with prominent eyes	5
Fringe – the hair completely covering the face	15
Shoulders and sides	15
Texture – silky	20
Density	15
Sweep – length of fullness, the hair flowing over the hindquarters	15
Condition	5
Size	5
Presentation	5

THE REX-COATED CAVY

This can be described as the woolly-coated guinea pig, a little like a teddy bear. The guard hairs are short, so the coat does not lie flat, but curls and stands upright. It has a springy feeling, when compared to other cavy coats. The colour is immaterial, it is the coat that counts.

A show animal must not have an extreme centre parting or a coat length greater than 1.3 cm (half an inch) and the usual rules of a broad head, large, well-spaced eyes and good, drooping ears apply.

ROANS AND DALMATIONS

These two varieties are not related but, for showing purposes, are usually classed together.

COAT TYPES

A smooth-haired cavy: The coat has an outer layer of coarse guard hairs, and a softer layer of undercoat.

Abyssinian: A series of rosettes and ridges are formed within the coat.

Rex: The coat runs from the rump to the head, making it stick out, and the coat should be groomed in this direction too.

COAT TYPES

This long-haired cavy has the added feature of a curly coat.

Black American Crested: The body is one colour, and the crest is another. In the English Crested, the body and crest are the same.

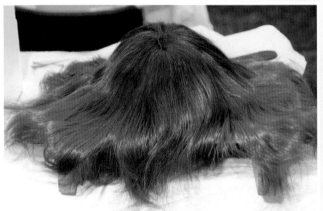

Peruvian: The coat has to be kept in wrappers apart from when the cavy is being shown.

138

SELF VARIETIES

Pink Eyed White: The ears are pink, and look like large rose petals.

Pink Eyed Golden: The coat should be the same colour as the face. In this example, the body is too dark.

Self-Red: This variety is less seen. The deep red colouring is very striking.

139

SELF VARIETIES

Self-Black: A glossy black coat with black shiny eyes.

Self-Chocolate: This cavy should be the colour of a dark chocolate bar – and the eyes should be ruby.

Cream Satin: This is a difficult colour to breed for.

NON-SELF VARIETIES

Dutch: This is a Chocolate Dutch cavy. The saddle line divides the body into two colours.

Silver Agouti: The emphasis on all six colours of Agoutis must be the quality of the ticking, colour, type and grooming.

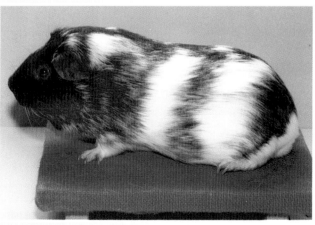

Black Magpie: The face is divided into two colours and there is a dividing line from the nose, down the back, up the middle of the stomach, through the mouth, and to the nose again.

141

NON-SELF VARIETIES

Black or Chocolate Harlequin: They are black/chocolate, yellow and brindling in a patchwork of colour along the sides and with a divided head.

Tortoiseshell and White: Seen from above, the clear sections of colour are easily seen.

Agouti Rex Bi-colour: This cavy is agouti and white.

142

NON-SELF VARIETIES

Chocolate Himalayan: A white body with darker, chocolate-coloured points on the ears, nose and feet.

Crested: A self coat with a different coloured crest.

Golden Satin: Due to the clarity of the glass-like hair and its ability to reflect the light, the Satin has a distinct gleam to its coat.

143

NON-SELF VARIETIES

Dalmation: This cavy has a spotted body, and the head has a blaze. The feet match the head colour.

Buff: Deep, rich buff shade, with no hint of lemon, apricot, or cream.

Side whisker fault: Visible at the side of the cheek, and looking like a wisp of twisted, erect hair, this is considered to be a serious fault.

The Roan is basically a black animal with white hairs evenly mixed throughout the body, but now some other colours have cleverly been incorporated through selective breeding. The strawberry roan is just such an example. This is a combination of red and white hairs. The solid colour should be confined to the head and feet, but white whiskers are not penalised when showing.

The Dalmation's head markings are a white blaze with a solid colour on either side. The feet are a solid colour. If your cavy lacks a blaze, and has spotting that is too heavy, uneven or too light, then showing is not an option.

Do not breed Dalmations and Roans together. The dangers are that the offspring will have almost non-existent eyes, and teeth problems. They rarely live to more than eight weeks.

The Standard for the Roan has **100 points** made up as follows:

Roan – mixing to be even throughout	30
Head – clean cut and solid black	20
Feet – solid black	10
Eyes (black, large and bold) and ears (black, set wide apart, large and drooping)	10
Coat and colour – short and silky, black and white	10
Size, type and condition	20

THE SATIN

This has the gloss-painted coat of the guinea pig world. Each individual hair has a glass-like quality. Consequently, the coat reflects the light and gives the animal a wonderful sheen. It should feel very fine, silky and even. Satins are usually bred in a smooth-coated colour.

There are also Crested Satins, a sort of American/English alliance, which gives the guinea pig a single crest on its head. They are controlled by the Rare Variety Cavy Club.

There are warnings with Satins. Never breed like to like, and they do not tend to have a long life span.

THE SHELTIE

This is the long-haired version of the smooth-coated guinea pig. So, it has no rosettes, but it does have a long train. Its hair sweeps back from its face.

Shelties can be sensitive about being groomed, particularly behind the shoulders. If your Sheltie is a pet, then clip the coat. The secret is to layer cut it, so that the rear end does not become soiled. The animal will be short-haired at birth, but the coat starts to grow very quickly.

If you are showing it, then wrappers are required, plus lots of care and attention to the coat. Don't try to show a Sheltie that does not like being brushed.

The Standard for the Sheltie divides into **100 points** as follows:

Head – broad with short nose and large, prominent eyes; with hair lying towards the rump; ears petal shape, set slightly drooping with good width between. — 15

Mane – sweeping back to join with sweep and is not parted — 15

Shoulders – broad with hair of a good length and density continuing evenly around sides — 20

Coat – silky texture and density — 20

Sweep – length and fullness of hair falling over hindquarters (sweep generally to be longer than the sides, which should be even in length) — 20

Condition and presentation – to be presented with no parting — 10

THE TEXEL

Texels may be shown in any colour or colour combination. With the coat, the sweep should be longer than the sides, with the length and fullness of hair falling over the hindquarters. To be presented with a central parting and an unmatted coat.

A crest or rosette appearing on a Texel will result in disqualification by the judge.

THE SMOOTH TORTOISESHELL AND WHITE

This is a very striking and beautiful guinea pig but it is extremely difficult to breed one that conforms to showing standards, now matter how good the breed stock. The patches of colour must be clean-cut, with no blurred edges.

This cavy has a smooth coat, which is a patch-work of red, black and white. The aim is to get each patch as square as possible, with straight lines between them, and the opposing patches on each side of the body should be of a different colour. The whole should add up to a beautifully symmetrical quilt.

If your Tort and White has breeching, which is where one colour runs right around the rump; banding, where one colour goes all the way round the body; or brindling, where patches of colour intermingle, do not show it.

146

The **100 points** for the Standard are attributed as follows:

Patches – clean cut, clear and distinct	25
Equal distribution and uniform placing of patches	25
Colours – black, red and white	20
Shape and size	15
Eyes and ears	5
Coat and condition	10

TRI-COLOURS

These guinea pigs are rather like the Tort and White but in different colours and they have three patches. The combinations are, for example, chocolate/cream/white and golden agouti/golden/white. Lilac/golden/white is also often seen.

The Standard for the Tri-colour is:

Patches – clear and distinct	45
Eyes – large and bold	10
Coat	10
Size, shape and condition	20
Colour – any three colours	15

(other than black/white/red, which is Tortoiseshell and White)

5. RARER VARIETIES

THE ALPACA

Alpacas may be shown in any colour or mixture of colours. The coat must be soft and springy with even, undamaged ends. The show Alpaca must be presented with a parting, and the coat must be unmatted so that a comb can pass through easily. The head of the Alpaca should be short and broad, with bright eyes and drooping, well-set ears.

THE HARLEQUIN

The head of the Harlequin should be half black and half yellow, divided down the centre of the face. The body should have an equal distribution of black and yellow and black/yellow mixture – three colours on each side in equal balance. The eyes should be large, dark and round, and the ears large, well set and drooping. A show pig with any white on the body, white leg or a large white patch on the head will be disqualified. The Chocolate Harlequin has chocolate in place of the black.

147

THE MAGPIE
The Magpie's head is half black, half white, divided down the centre of the face like the Harlequin. The three colours to be seen on each side of the body are equally balanced black, white and black/white mixture. There is no ruling on the colour of the feet. They can be any of the three colours. The Chocolate Magpie has a chocolate colour in place of the black.

THE MERINO
This pig has a soft and springy coat, which can be shown in any colour or combination of colours. The head rosette must be deep with only a pinpoint centre – a judge will penalise a pig with an open-centred rosette. The Merino must be presented with a parting and the hair must be unmatted and easily combable.

THE RIDGEBACK
It was often seen in Southern Cavy shows in the 1980s and photographs of them appear in books around that period. They have recently reappeared, and are under the Rare Variety Club (with a proposed guide standard). It is a smooth-coated cavy with a ridge of hair standing erect along the centre of the back from the base of the neck to the hips.
  The coat should be smooth and short; no longer than 1 inch (2.5 cm). Two rosettes only are permitted, which form the ridge. Any colour is permitted. Side whiskers constitute disqualification.

THE SABLE
This guinea pig should have a chocolate colour on its back, shading gently to beige or cream on the belly.

THE SLATE
This is a short, cobby pig with a solid slate blue colour that is carried down to the skin. Blue pigmentation of the feet, ears and nostrils is a plus.

TANS AND FOXES
The publishers are indebted to **Tony Cooke** for the following contribution on Tans and Foxes:
  For more than 70 years, people were struck by the fact that there were no Black Tans in the Cavy fancy. After all, mice had them, so did rabbits, and even dogs (Dobermann, Dachshund, Rottweiler, etc) so

why shouldn't we? In early 1998, they were finally found in Switzerland. A local fancier had bought one that she had found in a pet shop, and showed it under a UK judge, who recognised its importance. Arrangements were made for importation into the UK. They arrived in mid-1999 and were 'launched' at Bradford Championship in January 2000. Since then, they have spread right across Europe and to the USA and Philippines.

Breeding is the same as in fancy mice, since the tan gene is 'dominant' over the self. So, to start a strain of tans, you only need one specimen and can breed them with available self-colours, such as black, chocolate, beige or lilac. Babies without the characteristic tan belly are not carrying the tan gene, but any that have the correct belly colour are suitable for further breeding.

The breed characteristics are: a chestnut tan belly with a straight line demarcation between it and the top colour, tan eye circles, tan 'pea spots' (these are roughly where we have eyebrows), and the rump and flanks are 'ticked' with tan-tipped long hairs to give a very attractive overall effect.

It was soon clear that the Black Tan gene behaved exactly the same as in mice and rabbits, so, theoretically, it was possible to produce 'Foxes' from tans – and, sure enough, before long they were produced. In the case of the Fox family of colours, all red pigment is missing from the coat. This means that they have a pure white belly, white eye circles and 'pea spots', together with white ticking down the flanks and on the rump.

They are very striking indeed and have rapidly spread and become popular in a range of top colours, including black (which is, for historical reasons known as Silver Fox), chocolate and lilac.

Foxes were a bit slower in being distributed in the early days, because they are not so simple to produce by means of an outcross. With the tan, you will get quick results using a Self-Black sow, the corresponding outcross for the Fox is the 'dilute' (i.e. poor Self-Black, which comes out of Silver Agouti breeding), and these are not commonly available or identifiable. So the best way forward, if you want to breed Foxes, is to buy a trio from a breeder who already has them established.

TEDDIES
Rare Varieties has not issued guidance on this cavy at the time of going to print. Contact the club secretary for up-to-date information.

149

CHAPTER 10

BREEDING CAVIES

1. Principles of breeding
2. The pregnant sow
3. The birth
4. The nursing sow
5. Weaning
6. Cavy orphans
7. The frightened mother

Breeding cavies as pets or for exhibition can be an immensely rewarding and pleasurable experience. But first things first: you may have had other concerns than the sex of your pet when you first acquired it. Now is the time to make a careful examination to establish beyond doubt the sex of your cavies.

1. PRINCIPLES OF BREEDING

To establish whether a cavy is a boar or a sow, hold the cavy with your right hand across the chest and place your thumb and forefinger around the neck. With the cavy's shoulders against your chest, rest the rump in your cupped left hand so that the stomach faces upwards. The sex organs can now be examined clearly.

If your cavy is a male, you will notice that there is a rounded area in front of the anus. Beneath here is where the penis in encased, along with the internal scrotum. If you apply gentle pressure just above this area, the penis will protrude.

If your cavy is a female, you will see a shape like an inverted Y of hairless skin above the anus. This covers the vagina. In front of the vagina there is a very small slit; this is the opening of the urethra.

150

When sexing a guinea pig, do not be alarmed if some faeces are passed as this is quite a normal occurrence.

WHEN TO BREED

Although a pet guinea pig can breed from only a few weeks of age, you should wait until your sow is six months old before mating. The weight of the sow should be around 1.25 kg to 1.75 kg (1 1/2 to 2 lb). The boar should be eight months of age before mating. Waiting until this time has elapsed for both male and female cavies is necessary because breeding too early can result in health problems for both sexes, and can result in any litter being made up of weak and vulnerable babies.

A breeding pair needs to be in good overall condition – and not overweight. Small, stunted parents will more often than not have babies that are of poor quality.

There is a lot of nonsense talked about the 'mystery' of the cavy mating, with some owners claiming they only mate at night, hidden in their hutches.

THE BREEDING CYCLE

A sow cavy will come into season roughly every 18 days, when she will accept a mating for a matter of hours. If the sow is making a call rather like a purring noise (the mating call), she may mate immediately. Smell plays an important role in the mating of cavies, and you will usually observe the male sniffing the female's sex organs. Parts of her sex organs enlarge and become limp. The hymen membrane between them no longer forms a seal and the boar is allowed to penetrate.

Once a series of acts of mating has occurred, the boar will terminate matters by producing a waxy core that blocks up the sow's vagina. With this in place, there will be no more mating activity until after the litter is born and the sow comes into season again. The hymen re-seals itself until the litter arrives between 65 and 70 days after mating.

At one time it was considered necessary to take into consideration the seasons of the year. Guinea pig owners were told to start the matings from January onwards until mid-summer. When the spring arrives, so do masses of green herbage, which are very good for milk production in the sow. Litters born in the autumn and winter used to be slow in growing and lacking in stamina compared with the ones that appear in spring and summer. Nowadays, however, cavies that are kept in hutches indoors with a temperature fairly constant throughout the year, and that have the right kind of food, will be able to produce healthy litters all year round.

BREEDING FOR SHOW
Many different considerations come in to play when we are discussing breeding cavies for showing purposes. The first of these are in-breeding, line-breeding and out-crossing.

IN-BREEDING
With in-breeding, matings take place between cavies that are closely related. In the first instance, an owner looking to breed good-quality show cavies would purchase a sow and a boar that show excellent qualities for that particular breed. These two are mated, and then the resulting daughters are mated with the father and the sons mate with the mother. In some instances the litter sisters are mated with their brothers, but this type of mating is only used to try to correct a fault if all other attempts have failed. In-breeding can correct a fault that appears in the lineage.

LINE-BREEDING
Here we again have the mating of closely related cavies, but to a totally different plan. A stud is established of cavies that have good conformation to the breed standards. They are all interbred, but any cavy that bears a bad fault must be removed. The cavies that have better quality will then be bred on for the good points.

OUT-CROSSING
With the out-crossing method, the in-breeding method has failed to get rid of a fault in the cavies and an outsider of good quality that has no relationship to the existing cavies is brought in to try to 'breed out' the fault. Out-crossing will often produce a very pleasing show exhibit in the first litter of pure-breds.

BREEDING RECORDS
It is very important to keep a proper history of the breeding stock. Because a cavy's hock or heel is so slim, it cannot wear a leg ring for identification as is done for rabbits – the ring would easily slip off. So you will have to make a hutch card for each cavy that you breed. Print neatly on the card the cavy's name (and/or number), its breed, the date of its birth, the sire and dam details – then leave space for some notes on that particular cavy.

Cross reference these details to a stud book. This essential book of record will be a vital aid to the correct planning of your breeding programme.

BREEDING PROCEDURE

It is not necessary to wait for a sow to come into season (established through examination) before introducing the male. The practical and most natural thing to do is to let the sow and boar live together until the sow becomes pregnant. Keep them together for 36 days. During this time the sow will come into season twice, and if a mating does not occur in the first spell of being in season, then it most probably will during the second cycle.

To establish if the sow is pregant, a small examination will be required. Hold the female round her shoulder with one hand and slide your other hand under her to the lower, more soft and flexible part of the body. When the sow is five weeks pregnant, you should feel the young moving. At six week, the bones of the young start to become very pronounced.

After establishing that the sow is indeed pregnant, the best idea is to let her live on her own, away from the boar. If they are left together, a mating might well occur very soon after the litter is born, and this can result in the babes being trampled and crushed – sometimes to death. Then if the sow has to rear her young whilst being again pregnant, then her health could well be at risk.

Whether your sow is to be a pure-bred or a pet, she deserves rest between breeding. Some people say that a good sow is capable of producing five litters in 12 months, but this puts a terrible strain on the animal. The sow should be able to have a rest and be able to regain condition before a return to the breeding pen. Aim for two or three litters a year, and if one of the litters is large, then let the sow rest for more than a month before breeding again. After breeding a litter, it is normal for the sow to have grown quite noticeably.

Litters that have been properly planned from a pet cavy will give much interest and pleasure as they develop. But now you must think ahead. If you are overstocked with cavies, many problems can occur in coping with the increase in numbers. It is wise to find good homes for your surplus cavies to go to – but you must make sure that the new owners can properly care for their charges. It is sad but true that many people take home guinea pigs after reading a small advertisement in the paper or on a notice board with scant knowledge of how they should treat their new pets. They may pass from careless owner to careless owner, they may perish from being handled incorrectly. So make sure that your 'surplus' cavies will have considerate, sensible owners.

If you are breeding in a serious way for show, a number of sows will be required, of the highest quality of the breed you can find. The sows will be divided in breeding pens, in the following combinations:
• A pair: a boar and a sow
• A trio: two sows and a boar
• A pen: three or more sows and a boar

You can house up to six sows with one boar, but please note that you should never house more than one boar in a pen. Fighting is almost inevitable, and this can result in multiple deaths among the cavies. With multiple cavies in one pen, always attach all their hutch cards to the pen. An individual cavy will have some characteristic that you can identify and put on the card so that you know who is who.

2. THE PREGNANT SOW

The sow should be removed from the pen as soon as pregnancy is established. She is now what cavy breeders call 'in pig'. The sow should be put in a separate hutch with her hutch card attached. Some cavy enthusiasts will leave several pregnant sows together, if they become pregnant at roughly the same time, claiming that it is not necessary to isolate individual mothers-to-be. This is not a good idea, however, as it is likely that one or other of the sows will give birth ahead of the rest, and this can cause the other sows to start giving birth prematurely, resulting in weak or even stillborn babies. Even if all the sows give birth at the right time, there are problems ahead. Some sows will let the young of others suckle her, others will reject babies that are not their own, and the situation could end up with confusion and the inability to correctly identify the young of a particular sow. At this point the breeding records obviously become compromised. So a separate hutch for the new mother is the best policy.

Another quite common practice is to replace the pregnant sows in the breeding pen with sows that are ready for breeding. In these cases the new entrant to the pen must be watched carefully, as fighting can occur between her and the sows already in the pen. A boar will often come between sows that are fighting and stop them, but sometimes a sow can turn on a boar. Be very careful if you try to separate fighting cavies as you could easily end up being bitten. Continuous disturbances and fighting can cause miscarriages, and bites can turn into abscesses. The way to break the cycle of violence is to take a sow that is quarrelling with another sow away from that particular breeding pen and put her with another boar.

ABORTED PREGNANCIES

On occasion, a sow may be in the breeding pen for several months and still not become pregnant. Watch such a sow for traces of blood on her nose, as this could indicate that she has miscarried and has cleaned herself after the event. Also watch for signs of a bloody discharge from the vagina. A sow who had aborted will not display signs of illness such as loss of appetite (as we have said elsewhere, one of the first signs of illness in a cavy).

The sow will have miscarried around the 36th day of pregnancy and will usually re-mate on the same day as the miscarriage. To prevent the whole thing happening again, house the sow on her own after the miscarriage and mating to give her a chance to rest and go the full term. If she loses the babies again, it is likely that the sow has a weakness of the womb that will not allow her to go the full term of pregnancy, and of course such a pig should not be kept as a breeding sow.

INFERTILITY IN CAVIES

Some sows have big fertility problems that mean they never become pregnant, or produce only one baby a year, causing setbacks for the serious breeding programme. An infertile boar can set the breeding programme back many months, as mating calls from the sow followed by what appears to be a standard mating from the boar will lead you to believe all is well. It is only when none of the sows in the breeding pen become pregnant over time that you begin to suspect something is amiss. At this point there is an examination that you can carry out to establish if there is an anatomical fault in the boar that is causing the problem. Is the boar on the large size? Sometimes, extra large boars are infertile.

Carry out the examination as if you were trying to sex the male, as shown earlier. Press on the abdomen to provoke the penis to protrude. Once the penis is extended, look at the tip for two prongs or horns. If these horns are uneven in length, or one of the horns is missing, your boar will mate but will be incapable of fertilising the sow. Some boars do not have this fault but are just naturally sterile.

BREEDING SETBACKS

There can be many obstacles to be faced in establishing cavy breeding as a serious and successful hobby. The new breeder might feel challenged by some of the difficulties and disappointments that will occur. Sometimes the breeder may feel like giving up the practice altogether because of a succession of reverses. Remember that the successful breeder needs a combination of determination and patience to win through in the end, and when success does come it is a tremendously rewarding experience.

Apart from those already discussed, other setbacks in cavy breeding are:

1) The strain of a very heavy pregnancy may kill a sow only a few days ahead of her due date for giving birth.
2) Cold, damp or drafty cages may cause a pregnant sow to go into decline very quickly and die.
3) The sows may have difficult births during which the young arrive with the back feet first rather then the head.
4) Even more serious is a birth where the first baby arrives with its nose tucked under its body. This baby will die as will all the others that follow.
5) An entire litter may be neglected at birth and all the young may die.
6) Disruption of a breeding programme when a boar that has died cannot be replaced by a boar of the correct lineage.

THE GESTATION PERIOD

Gestation can take from 65 to 70 days after conception has taken place. If the in-pig sow is carrying a litter of average size, her condition will be noticeable at about four weeks. She will increase in size quickly and should be handled as little as possible. A cavy has a very flexible frame and the lower body is particularly vulnerable to injury, so the wrong sort of handling can easily induce a miscarriage with possibly fatal consequences.

From the time the sow starts to show her pregnancy, she will rest for much of the time. She should be supplied with plenty of water, fresh vegetables and dry food. Be careful not to give too much dry food. Half the amount usually given is recommended, otherwise the sow will put on too much weight and may face a difficult birth as a result.

A nest need not be provided for the sow and her litter. The babies do not need the protection of many other creatures at birth because they are not born naked but are covered in hair. They babies are really tiny versions of their parents, complete with teeth, claws, whiskers and open eyes. The average cavy litter has four babies, although six is not uncommon. If there are more, often a couple of babies are stillborn.

Babies born before the 60th day of pregnancy are premature and will be weak and small. Hair will just be seen growing through the skin – diagnostic of premature birth. The premature birth will take its toll on the sow, who will often go to the corner of the hutch and sit quietly covering her offspring until she has recovered the strength lost through the shedding of blood through the miscarriage.

3. THE BIRTH

The gestation period sees the babies enveloped in a membrane and protected by fluid. As her labour pains begin, she will strain continually with the contractions. The first baby's head will be pushed through the vaginal opening by the force of her contractions. When the nose of the baby appears, the sow bends to bite through the membrane. The fluid surrounding the baby is released and the baby should start to breathe on its own. If the membrane is not broken, then the baby will certainly suffocate to death. The failure of the mother to break the membrane is a major cause of death in the young. Some keepers of cavies think that the babies are stillborn, when in fact they have been born live and have died because the membrane was not breached.

If an owner is present when the birth takes place, then he or she can help if the membrane around a baby remains intact. Without delay, gently break the membrane over the nose of the baby, open the mouth and blow short, rapid breaths into the mouth. While you are doing this, move the back legs of the baby so that energy is exerted to get the heart pumping and the lungs working. There is hope that the bay will survive if it gasps for breath. At this stage it is vital that you keep the baby warm, so cup it in your hands and continue to blow down the throat. A cloth should be used to gently dry the coat. Hopefully, the baby will now start to squeak. Continue to provide warmth, but avoid giving it anything to drink.

After it has shown signs of life, you can provide a hot-water bottle wrapped in a cloth. Put the bottle along the side of the hutch or box. Do not put the baby on the bottle – it may be too hot. If your life-saving efforts have proved successful, you will see the baby start to recover in under two hours. It will show its strength by standing up, and at this point it should be re-united with its mother. Put the baby under her and see if she will accept it – there is a possibility that she will reject it because she hasn't cleaned the baby and therefore will not recognise it.

Most of the time, happily, the mother will have released the membrane round the baby and will be making encouraging noises as she cleans and dries her baby. She will eat the membrane and afterbirth. The afterbirth will sometimes be found lying in the hutch if the sow has not had the strength to dispose of it in the normal way, but usually you will be presented with a clean hutch with maybe just a few bloodstains on the floor, and a nice litter of small hairy babies to admire.

The mother will continue to clean a baby until it stands up and utters little cries. It will be hungry, and will snuggle close to its mother and begin to suckle. When all the babies have been through the cleaning routine, a mother may well nudge them into the corner of the hutch and then lay her body directly in front of them, keeping them warm.

If you are breeding to show, you will need to make an examination of the babies in the very early stages. Gently press around the edges of the ears of the babies so that any creases disappear. In a cavy that is bred for exhibiting, crumpled ear is a fault. Gently pressing out the ears on the day of birth will remedy this fault. Apart from this, do not disturb the babies further. It is possible that they will take fright and rush around the hutch – this may cause them to stay away from the mother and litter brothers and sisters and get cold, causing health problems.

As a day or two goes by, you will observe that the babies lie on their backs as the mother continually licks their genital areas. This stimulates the babies into passing urine and faeces. If this stimulation does not take place, the babies may well not start passing waste and can die as a result.

It is the norm for a sow to make a caring and devoted mother to her babies. There are cases, however, when the mother will reject a baby, nudging it away from her as it is trying to suckle. The mother may move the other babies into a corner and keep the rejected one away. This type of behaviour, of course distressing to observe, is usually an indication that there is something wrong with the baby. It may be deformed in a way that means it will not thrive, or it may be blind, or too weak to ultimately survive. It is a very unhappy sight to observe a blind baby cavy going round and round in circles, trying to find the mother that has rejected it. No matter how many times you try to re-introduce a blind baby to its mother, the sow will have none if it and will just keep rejecting this unsighted offspring as before.

A couple of other hazards to watch out for: a mother through over-zealous cleaning, may damage a baby's ears or toes. Also, she may have inadvertently injured the body with her teeth if the baby had become stuck while exiting the sow's body.

4. THE NURSING SOW
A sow has but two milk glands and teats, these are located at the base of the thighs. So if there are more than two babies, they are obliged to take turns at feeding. Try to make sure that bigger, more dominant, babies do not prevent their weaker siblings from feeding. In the case of a large litter where some babies are clearly not getting their share of milk, then diluted milk on a spoon may be given to them by the breeder – see the section ahead on Cavy Orphans. Another substitute for the mother's feeding is to give bread and milk in a bowl. The bread should first be softened in hot water then drained, and diluted milk added. Undiluted cow's milk is not a good idea. It can easily go sour and upset the baby's stomach. Diluted canned evaporated milk can be given.

A breeder must keep a close eye on a sow with four or more babies. What to look for is a weakening of her condition at around three weeks after the birth of the litter, due to too much demand being placed on lactation. A sign of distress is for the sow to utter little cries because her teats are being bitten because of low milk production. This is a serious sign, as damage to the teats, if it goes unchecked, can lead to permanent deformities, which will affect the sow's ability to feed her young in future. The only thing to be done is to take the babies away from the mother. A sow so weakened will take a considerable time to rest and recover her condition.

5. WEANING
The baby cavies learn to cope with solid foods very quickly – remember that they do have the advantage of being born with teeth. They will be taught how to eat solid food by their mother, who will present the huddled group of babies with tasty morsels of bread, roots, grass and vegetables. It is common to see the babies starting to eat at 24 hours old. It is important that the breeder provides the sow with plenty of nourishing food – don't forget fresh vegetables – three times a day during the period that the babies are suckling.

All being well, the babies will start to grow rapidly from four days onwards. They will usually stay by their mother until they are a month old. This is the time to remove the boar babies from their mother and siblings. At one month of age, a boar is very virile and capable of mating with his mother and sisters. The little sows can come into season at any time after one month of age. There is a case for removing a boar that is making disturbances at three weeks of age – he could be bitten on the ear, rendering him useless for exhibitions.

The young females can stay with their mother until lactation is finished. However, if you are intending to remove all the litter at once, check the mother's milk glands to make sure they are not hard and swollen with milk. If they are, then it is best to allow the babies to drain off the milk by suckling. Leaving a sow with excess milk is dangerous because inflammation called mastitis can set in – even abscesses may form. If by some chance you have let her litter go to new homes and a sow's milk glands are hard and swollen, then she should be taken off all green food for two days (this will cut down on milk production) but make sure plenty of water is provided.

After weaning, keep the young sows you are going to retain together. Do not allow boars to live together after three months because they will fight viciously. When the breeding season is over, select the well-grown young boars and sows that you will be using to breed from in the next season.

6. CAVY ORPHANS
It is indeed a sad event when a mother dies leaving a litter of babies. Some breeders will have the litter destroyed, but many will try other alternatives.

FOSTER MOTHERS
If a breeder has a sow with babies that are a day or two old, it is worth seeing if the sow will act as a foster mother to the orphaned babies. Take the foster mother from her hutch and place her in a small box that is complete with bedding. Leaving the mother in the hutch can mean that she will keep wandering about and her new charges will not settle with her. Once the sow is in the box, take all but one of her own babies from her, and keep them warm. Then rub the newcomers against those babies, so that they pick up their smell. Then introduce the newcomers to the box. The sow will then give her verdict: if she starts to clean the babies and make encouraging noises, then they are likely to be accepted. The sign of rejection from the sow takes the form of her putting her nose underneath the newcomers and nudging them away. An hour should be enough time for you to see if the newcomers

are allowed to suckle from the foster mother. Then you can return the rest of the original litter to her. Take all the cavies to the hutch where they will huddle together to keep warm and take turns suckling. In the coming days, be careful and make sure that all the combined brood are getting their fair share of mother's milk, and the babies have started experimenting with eating solids.

DOING IT YOURSELF

If the fostering does not work because of rejection by the sow, then it is worth having a go at trying to save the orphans yourself – time and patience will be required. Warmth is one of the keys to success. Place a hot-water bottle in a shoebox, siting it on the inside wall of the box rather than putting at the bottom. If it is at the bottom of the box, you will have to disturb the babies every time the bottle needs refilling. Find some old warm materials, such as old woollen socks or scarves for the babies to be on or under. If you wish, you can make a small hide of hay to place in the corner of the box, which will give the babies something to nibble as well as providing warm shelter.

Once the babies have settled in, they can be given a drink of canned evaporated milk mixed with water (one part evaporated milk to three parts water). As we have said before, undiluted cow's milk is too strong for the babies.

When you are ready to give the feed, wrap the baby in a warm cloth, which will make it easier to hold. Feed a few drops of the milk mixture via a small spoon tilted towards the baby's mouth. It is important for the baby to suck the milk itself, so be patient. If you try to force the milk down the baby's throat, it could well come back into the nose and go down into the lungs, with serious consequences. Using an animal feeding bottle can have similar bad results.

This spoon feeding should keep the little ones happy. They will need a feed every couple of hours – sometimes one an hour – during daytime for the first two days. Giving a feed late at night and making sure they are warm should mean that they will be fine until the next morning. Be sure to wash around the babies' mouths after feeding, and to make sure no milk has spilt on to their coats, as having a sticky coat is anathema to a cavy. You must also wipe the anus and genitals with a clean, damp cloth – this mimics the mother's habit of licking them in these areas to stimulate the passing of faeces.

Teaching the babies to eat solids is not easy – they do not readily understand how to pick up food. The best way to encourage them is to put a young but maturing cavy in with the babies. The babies learn to eat by observing the slightly older cavy, but be watchful and make sure the older cavy's behaviour is gentle. The babies can have hay, crushed oats, bread, little pieces of grass and some dilute-milk and bread mixture. It is best to keep the babies inside your home for the first ten days or so, where they will be easier to care for.

THE FRIGHTENED MOTHER
Even though she may have partially cleaned her babies, suddenly a mother may appear to become extremely scared of her offspring and try to hide from them. If you place the babies near her, she will shriek and appear terrified. Somehow, she seems not to recognise what these strange, wet creatures are and will stay away from them – leaving the offspring to become dangerously chilled.

The best way to cope with this problem is to follow the foster mother route and put the sow in a small box with bedding and slowly introduce the young. This is best done in the home if the birth took place in an outside hutch. Hold the mother so she can smell each of the babies individually, then place her in the small box – the sow may probably still be kicking up a fuss and shrieking at this point. Then start putting the babies under her one by one. After a little time has elapsed, she should start the routine of making encouraging sounds and cleaning the babies as she recognises what they are. Once she seems content with the babies and they start to suckle, the whole group can be returned to the hutch. Make sure the mother settles with the babies before you feed her again.

If the attempt fails and the mother will not take to the babies, try following this method for suckling them if you have a sow who is suckling a little less than ten days old. Sit down with a towel on your lap and hold the sow on her rump with her teats exposed. Hold a baby and put its mouth to one of the teats and let it suck from the sow. If the baby is having difficulty, encourage the milk flow by gently squeezing the teat. The baby will soon get the idea as it tastes the milk, and will begin sucking. You can check that the baby is sucking by studying carefully the sides of its mouth: you will see its hairs there moving as it swallows.

CHAPTER 11

SHOWING YOUR CAVY

1. Entry form
2. Ear labels
3. Judging table and book
4. Show grooming
5. The art of wrapping

The first steps towards exhibiting your cavy should take you to a show to learn at first hand how it all works. People in the cavy fancy are usually friendly folk who will encourage the novice and will share information with them. Some exhibitors will have been showing cavies for a lifetime and have built up a fund of knowledge that is invaluable. But don't be intimidated by the experience of others – very soon you will be making your mark on the cavy show world, with a little help from your new-found friends.

A Pen Show is a large, all-day affair, usually starting at 10.30 am, with two or more judges. These shows are organised by fanciers who belong to cavy clubs. Someone who wishes to join a club should approach the secretary and, on acceptance, an annual membership fee will be paid and the new member will be given a handbook and a separate breeds book, which features detailed information on the Breed Standards for all pure breeds.

These form the Holy Grail for breeders to aspire towards, and the many things that judges need to assess. The handbook also contains the rules that all exhibitors must abide by.

A newcomer to the world of showing can find out much information about where and when the shows are by consulting the various websites and publications listed at the back of this book.

Secretaries of shows send out schedules and all entries must be paid for. The schedule sets out the classification of various breeds, identifies the judge and gives a closing date for entries. Ask the secretary for advice as to which classes you should enter.

To get started, the novice exhibitor should take their cavy to Pet Show held at the same time as a Pen Show. This will be a learning experience for the new exhibitor and the cavy as well. You will learn the various procedures for showing and your cavy will be able to adjust to large numbers of people, strange noises and handling on the judge's table.

The show's schedule contains a large number of abbreviations that you must be able to recognise. They may appear thus:

A.C.	Any Colour
A.O.C.	Any Other Colour
A.V.	Any Variety
A.O.V.	Any Other Variety
A.A.	Any Age
B or S	Boar or Sow
Ad.	Adult
D.	Duplicate
U/5 mos.	Under five months
Intermediate 5/8 mos.	Over five months but under eight months

Here is an example of the classes shown in cavy clubs:

Selfs (all one colour): i.e. White, Cream, Black, AOC, also 5-8 months and 3-5 months

Non Selfs: Abyssinian, Rough-haired, Long-haired, Crested, also 5-8 months and 3-5 months

Ticked and Marked: Agouti, Dalmation, Roan, Himalayan, Dutch, Tortoiseshell and White, A.O.V, also 5-8 months and 3-5 months

There will also be classes for Rare Varieties, Junior Pure Breeds and Pet classes for adult and junior exhibitors.

1. ENTRY FORM

The first space on an entry form, which must be sent in ahead of the show, is for the pen number of the cavy, issued by the secretary. The second space is the breed class. The third space is for use by the duplicate classes. The fourth space is the cavy's description. The fifth space is for the entry fee.

Let us say you want to exhibit a Self-White sow under five months of age. Look on the show's entry form to see if there is a class for its own colour, as it must go into its breed class first. If there is not a class for Self-White, it must go into the class covering any Self Any Colour under 5 months. If you do not feel that your cavy is an outstanding exhibit, you need not duplicate it into any other class. Suppose that you also want to exhibit a Roan Abyssinian adult boar. If there is no class for its colour, you must enter him in A.O.C. Abyssinian Adult. If he is a very good specimen, you can enter him in Challenge A.V. Adult classes. A Red Dutch sow with only average markings need not be duplicated at all; it will just go in to its breed class.

Should you find that a separate class for your Self cavy is not available, you must keep it as a Self with its breed in the A.O.C. In the case of the Agouti, Himalayan and Peruvian, if there is not a breed class, they must be entered in the A.O.V. of the Non-Self section.

When you have filled in the entry form, send it to the secretary with the proper fees before the closing date – although it is possible to pay at the show.

At your first show, do not enter your cavy into every duplicate class that is applicable. As a new fancier, you may think that you have an outstanding cavy and will not notice some of the faults that a judge will. It would be very disappointing for you to have your cavy placed very low in its class after you had been thinking that it was so special. If it were to be placed very low in the class, it would not be awarded a prize in the duplicate classes where all breeds meet, because entries from other classes would be placed over it after they had won prizes in their own classes. You must learn by experience. If your cavy gets on quite well in its first show, then the duplicating can be extended at the next show. You must remember that the judges' opinions differ with exhibits; one judge may put a cavy down in the awards and the next judge may place it quite high.

2. EAR LABELS

What happens on arrival at the show? Having previously sent your entry form to the secretary, go to the person who is distributing ear labels at the show. Give your name if you are not known and you will be given your entry form with stick-on numbered ear labels, corresponding to each breed class in which your cavy has been entered. Stick the small ear labels securely on the outside of the cavy's ear and put the cavy in the pen with the same number. Give your cavy a little hay and some food in the pen.

3. JUDGING TABLE AND BOOK

The judging table is the same for all shows. Judging tables are set up and covered with sheeting. A small stool or box is used for sitting the cavy on for assessing all-round quality before close examination. The box is placed close to the judging pens that are on the judging table.

Judging pens were introduced to the cavy fancy by R.T.R. Elward These pens are like open-topped boxes joined together, usually 6 inches (15 cms) high, 7 inches (18 cms) wide, and have a low front of three inches (8 cms). One box accommodates one cavy while the class is being judged. The judging pens were given the name of 'Honest Steward', meaning never leaving the judge.

It is the practice of some stewards to help until their classes are judged, then they disappear. It is poor stewarding when a judge has to call for stewards while he is in the middle of judging.

It is the duty of the stewards to look after the cavies on the table and to see that they are never unattended, especially when they are being returned to their pens. They also keep a watch on the ear labels and make sure that they do not come off as the cavy is brought to the table. The stewards also make certain that the cavies that are in the pens are put on the table in the numerical order that corresponds with the judging book. Only stewards are allowed to remove cavies from their pens once they have been penned.

As the cavies are placed on the judging table, their sex is noted in the judging book by the judge against the pen number – this is a great help in cases where an ear label falls off and the cavies are all the same colour. For example, just by noting the sex, the mix-up can be straightened out.

The judging book has a page made out for each class and will contain the pen numbers of each cavy entered in the appropriate classes. All of the judging is done by the number that the cavy wears on its ear. As the judge examines each cavy, notes are made in the judging book regarding the merit of the cavy.

After completion of a class, the judge signs the judging slip that tears from the book. Once he has signed this slip, the awards are final unless a mistake has been made. If the secretary and judge agree that a mistake has been made, then the award can be altered. The slip is then given to the secretary who then enters the awards against the names entered in the class.

The prize cards are displayed on the pens and the prize money paid out after all prize cards have been put on the pens.

4. SHOW GROOMING

When you first visit a cavy show, you may notice the types of cavies that received awards. A number of the smooth-coated cavies were well presented, meaning that the coat had been groomed, resulting in sleek appearance. Had they not been groomed, the coats would have appeared dull with hairs of uneven length over the top of the body.

Grooming and washing of the cavy are all that are allowed by the clubs. The rules state: "An exhibit has to be disqualified if, in the opinion of the judges, it has been subjected to practices calculated to deceive or to give false impression of merit." They must be exhibited in a perfectly natural condition.

When you are breeding cavies for exhibition, you look for show potential shortly after birth. From an early age, you handle your cavy frequently, to train it for the quietness he will need to display at shows. It has to learn to sit still on the judging table, not being held by the judge's stewards. It will be unable to show off its fine qualities if it is frightened and tries to run off the table.

A cavy of any variety must have a quiet disposition. It will stand little chance of winning if the judge is unable to sit it on a stool or grooming board on the judging table to assess its general qualities. This is required for any pure breed that is judged to standard rules.

To train your cavy to sit on a stool or grooming board, you should not begin the task at a distance too high from the ground. A chair (with a piece of burlap on the seat for the cavy to dig its toenails into) is a good training height; if your cavy falls from the chair, it is not so likely to get hurt from this height. You must take special care until the time that it can sit contentedly on the chair unattended. It is during training that a fall can cause a cavy's teeth to become broken. Gradually raise the height of the training level to a table of about $4^1/_2$ feet (1.5 metres), the equivalent of the judging table.

A cavy can also be trained to sit still by alternately petting it and setting it on a grooming board every day, so it can get used to the idea of sitting while not being petted.

GROOMING SMOOTH-COATED VARIETIES

First spray with Johnson's ant-mite sprat for pet birds. During the training to sit still, you can begin to groom your cavy. You do this in smooth-coated varieties by first stroking it from head to rump with both hands. After stroking, make long sweeps down the body with the sides of your thumb, preferably dampened using a sponge. These

167

sweeps are for taking out long guard hairs that protect the finer undercoat; if swept in this manner, the hair will not be patchy or uneven.

For the novice fancier, the art of grooming needs a lot of practice. It is best that you practice on a cavy that is not needed for exhibition so that the right pressure of the thumbs can be learned. At first, it can be just another set-back, as too much or too little grooming can make a cavy lose position or awards.

If your cavy is to be exhibited in an up-coming show, you should start to groom it about three weeks before the show. Excessive grooming in a short period of time causes a cavy to lose condition rapidly. Extended over three weeks or so, the cavy would then be back in firm condition.

When you are grooming, you must apply firm pressure by your thumb, otherwise the guard hairs will not come out. At this stage, your cavy's coat will look dull, dusty and thick because of the presence of dead hairs. These dead hairs are easily removed with a few sweeps of the thumb. You must also groom the sides or flank; do not forget the face, because the hairs on the face often look rather coarse. Make a few sweeps up from the nose through the forehead and cheeks and then go down the back. You must release some of the pressure in the centre as the hair in this part is always very thin. When over-groomed, this can produce an uneven appearance or bare patches in the skin; it will take about six weeks for the hair to grow back to full length. Be very careful when you go over the hipbones because you can easily catch your thumb here, causing bare patches over the rump. Sit your cavy so that nothing will interrupt the long sweeps that you will be making.

Go over the hair, sweeping it between your thumb and your first finger. If guard hairs still protrude, use a suede shoe brush or wear a rubber glove and apply it going crosswise for final touches in removing uneven hairs.

You should then hold your cavy on your hand and check for uneven side hairs and lower rump hairs that were hidden from you while your cavy was sitting on the chair. Go around these areas with your damp thumb and your first finger to groom them evenly.

Grooming is not an easy matter to learn from written instructions; it would be easier for you to watch an experienced fancier who could better explain the proper method. You would then see the correct way and amount of pressure to be used.

You will notice that your hands will get very dirty while you groom your cavy. This is just a combination of dust from sawdust, shavings, hay and grease from the cavy's hair.

Once your cavy has gained enough confidence to sit unattended on the chair, the next thing to do is to make a small wire-mesh pen (one foot square or 10 square cms) equivalent to a show pen. Put your cavy into this pen for a few hours a day. Feed him in the pen so that he becomes accustomed to being in the pen. When the time comes to take your cavy to a show and it is placed in a similar pen, it will not be frightened. As previously mentioned, anything strange to a cavy will likely frighten it.

Being shut in an exhibition box or carrying case can distress your cavy. If this occurs, when you arrive at the show it will be huddled in the corner of the box and will feel limp when you handle it. An exhibition cavy must be in firm condition, so it is best that you train it to overcome its fear of being enclosed. Place it in the carrying case for about an hour for the first day and then extend the time. When it has lost its fear of the case, give it some food so that it learns to eat in it for future trips to cavy shows.

The final preparation comes just one week before the show. Your cavy will need a bath to cleanse the hair and skin and to remove any mites and dirt from the coat. The mites are very small but they irritate the skin. Sometimes cavies are exhibited with mites, and pass them on to other cavies on the judging table. There is also another type of mite that appears like fine dust over the hair. The mite are passed from one cavy to another or come along with poor-quality hay. However, they do not live on human beings, cats or dogs.

Washing your cavy will take very little time. Some cavies are distressed on the first wetting but, after several minutes, are not upset by being in the water. You will need a plastic bowl with a piece of towelling in the bottom to prevent your cavy from slipping. Medicated shampoos should be used as they rid cavies of mites. They can even help kill off a special and nasty mite called the sarcoptic which mite, which burrows under the skin of a cavy, causing great distress.

Put about two inches (5 cms) of warm water in the bowl and thoroughly wet your cavy's hair. Apply the shampoo, working up a lather that spreads over the body. Wash the inside of the ears too, because mites congregate in them. Leave the shampoo on it for at least five minutes; if you wish, you can wrap it in a towel to keep it from shaking off the shampoo. Put your cavy back into the shampoo water; gently scrub the feet, between the toes, and the toenails with a nailbrush. With adult boars, the 'grease spot' at the tail stump section will need attention. This spot gets very dirty; if you miss it when you give him a bath, he will lose points when being judged. It is best to apply a washing-up liquid on the spot with your finger tip; let it soak into the grease for a few minutes, then use the nailbrush and the shampoo water and the spot should come clean.

You can now rinse you cavy in warm water and towel it dry. You can use a blow-dryer or put it in a box and keep it warm in the house until the hair dries. In the winter, do not return your cavy to an outside hutch until the following day. This prevents night-time chilling after being freshly washed. This risk can also be avoided by not keeping cavies in an outside hutch during winter.

Once the hair has settled down after washing and its natural sheen has returned, continue grooming the coat by using a piece of silk cloth and a bristled brush. Too soft a brush will only brush the top coat, but the under coat is also inspected.

Abyssinians will need their ears, feet and stomach cleaned prior to exhibiting. The harsh hair and the rosettes can be brushed with a stiff-bristled brush; the rosettes should be attended to singly. The crested variety needs the same body grooming as the smooth-coated variety; the crest on the forehead should be brushed with a toothbrush.

Always leave sufficient time before departing for a show to check your cavy's mouth, feet and stomach for overnight stains, and re-check on arrival at the show. Grooming and washing are not judged as giving a false impression of merit. In a variety with a thick coat, these steps have to be carried out, because of the possible presence of mites, grease, and dead hair.

It is not until a sleek coat has been obtained that a true top and undercolour are assured. It is a well-known adage that "the shorter the coat, the better the colour." Long coats show flakiness, meaning a lighter undercolour is seen because long hair does not carry its colour to the full extent of each hair.

Whatever the breed is that you exhibit, your aim is to win an award and to have your exhibit look its best. Your exhibit should not be ungroomed, dirty, in poor condition, have skin blemishes or carry mites.

GROOMING LONG-HAIRED VARIETIES
Peruvians, Shelties, Coronets, Alpaca, Merino and Texel.
The grooming and conditioning of all the long-haired varieties is totally different from the method used for the smooth varieties.

When your long-haired guinea pig is a few weeks old, you can begin to train it to be quiet and to get accustomed to being groomed.

When you groom your long-haired guinea pig, use a brush or a comb. You must have a separate brush or comb for each one of your long-haired cavies. If the scent from one cavy is passed on to another, it could result in one of them biting pieces out of its own hair to rid itself of the other's scent.

The hair, which will eventually be very long, grows at the rate of roughly one inch (2.5 cms) per month. With care, the hair can be kept in a showable condition for about 18 months to two years. Naturally, the cavy cannot trail this very long hair around in its hutch, so you just put it in wrappers (described later in this chapter).

Any long-haired variety should not be kept on sawdust or wood shavings as these can get into the coats and spoil them. The hay for eating should be kept in a tied-up bundle in the hutch. If you feel that a hay bedding is necessary, then the hay should be cut up into short lengths to stop your cavy from burrowing under it. By burrowing, the cavy would be spoiled for exhibition because the hair of the frontal or fringe, and the hair on the sides of the shoulders, would become dragged out.

When your long-haired cavy is about eight weeks old and is used to being brushed and is quiet, the rear sweep (the hair from the hindquarters) will then be a few inches long and will start to become urine-stained. This could spoil the hair. To prevent this damage, put the hair into a wrapper. Most fanciers place, in adults, a wrapper on each side, one on the rear sweep. These should not allow the hair to curl at the ends. The wrappers look like neat little parcels; once the hair is long, they are undone only for the cavy to be brushed or for presentation on the judging table.

The first time that you place a wrapper on your young cavy, it may scratch or bite it off, especially if it is rather tight and the hairs are being pulled. Always make sure that the wrapper is comfortable. If your cavy removes it, keep trying until it gets used to it. Some never get used to the wrapper and are not suitable for exhibition. If this is the case, use them for breeding stock and keep their hair clipped back.

To make a wrapper, you will need a piece of brown paper (some people use cotton cloth instead) that is three inches (7.5 cm) wide and four inches (10 cm) long. Fold it into three sections length-wise with one end turned over one-half inch (just over one centimetre) to make a fold. In the centre section, place a piece of balsa wood, three-quarters of an inch (2 cm) wide, under the folded end and seal the whole fold across so that the wood cannot slip out. (Some exhibitors do not use balsa wood at all.) Fold the sides into the middle so that the wrapper looks like a flat oblong and then fold it length-wise to make accordion pleats that are about one inch (2.5 cm) apart. The wrapper is now ready. As your cavy grows and the length of its hair increases, you will need to increase the size of the wrapper, too.

Place your cavy on a box or stool and make one parting down the centre of the back and another across the rump. The parting should resemble the letter 'T'. The head of the T takes the hair from the sweep; this is the only section that will need to be wrapped for a young cavy. When your cavy is four to five months old, it will also need to have a wrapper on each of the sides. The stroke of the letter T is the dividing line down the middle of the back. It takes the hair from the sides and includes the frontal, which is brushed to each side. The hair from the parting is then brushed down to the lower sides and is ready for wrapping.

Take the wrapper in one hand and the hair from the sweep in the other. Place the hair in the centre fold of the wrapper; make sure that the end of the wrapper that has no balsa wood in it is against your cavy's body. Turn the sides in and fold up the wrapper in accordion folds so that the end of the wrapper faces downwards, preventing sawdust and dirt from getting into it and damaging the hair. Secure the balsa wood and wrapper with an elastic band; it will appear to be a small parcel. This method is good for any long-haired cavy once its hair is long enough to wrap. (See also: The Art of Wrapping, page 173.)

To wash your long-haired cavy, you will need a bowl of warm water, three to four inches (7 to 10 cm) deep. Place a piece of towelling in the bottom of the bowl to prevent your cavy from slipping. Have the medicated shampoo, warm rinsing water and dry towels at hand. Unwrap your cavy's hair and brush it out. Place the cavy in the water and hold it with one hand at all times; if it should panic, it could get the back feet and toenails tangled in the wet hair and cause damage.

Never rub the shampoo in the hair for this will cause the hair to tangle. You should gently squeeze the coat after shampooing. Rinse your cavy several times with the warm water, then lift it out of the bowl and let the water drain off. Place it on a dry towel or on any absorbent material and pat the hair to remove the moisture.

Do not rub the hair with the towel because the tangling that results could damage the hair for exhibition. It is best to dry the hair with a hairdryer. Once you have completely dried the hair, you can brush it and put it back in the wrappers. Like any other cavy that has recently been washed, do not put it in an outside hutch immediately, but wait until the next day.

The habits of all long-haired cavies are very similar. One important thing for you to remember is that the young ones that show exhibition potential should be housed on their own soon after weaning because they often chew or nibble on each other's hair. Such damage to their hair would leave them suitable only for breeding stock.

Once either of these varieties is on the judging table, it is against the rules to brush their hair. You should, however, bring your cavy's brush to the judging table because the judge is allowed to brush the hair if it has been disarranged during the examination. Once the judging has commenced, any of the long-haired varieties are allowed to be brushed for presentation only. No other form of grooming may be used.

For grooming a Sheltie, the instructions differ somewhat only in the wrapping and in the brushing. The Sheltie's hair is brushed from the mane or head furnishing to the rear sweep, as it does not have a centre parting. Usually, only one wrapper is required and it is placed on the sweep. It fanciers wish, they also have wrappers on the sides.

The procedure for washing the Sheltie is the same as it is for all long-haired cavies.

5. THE ART OF WRAPPING

The grooming and wrapping of a long-haired cavy is something that beginners find a little bewildering. It is not easy, even when you are experienced, and especially if your cavy is in full coat or restless.

The purpose of wrapping is to keep the hair in perfect condition for show purposes. Therefore, just wrap the show stock and clip the coats of your breeding cavies. It is a good idea, however, to start brushing out several babies, then, if one chews its coat, or turns out not to be quite good enough, you have others to carry on with and do not have to start at the beginning.

From the time a long-haired show cavy has hair long enough to be wrapped, it must henceforth be wrapped at all times, except when in front of the judge or when being groomed. Many new fanciers think that they are just wrapped to go to shows, but they must be groomed every day, especially as the hair grows longer.

It is best for a beginner to start with a baby long-haired, and not buy an older cavy in show coat. You could ruin it in a day because of your inexperience. Each day, you should hold your very young cavies in your hand and stroke them from the tail-end towards the head. This will calm them down and get them used to being handled. As they grow older, put them on a board (something like a shoe box with a cloth on it will do at this stage), and brush them, still from the rear towards the head, with a baby brush (a soft bristle brush being better than nylon).

If you get any small knots in the coat, dampen them, and tease them out gently with your fingers, the tail of the comb, or a small knitting needle. Never comb them out, or you could remove a considerable amount of coat.

When your baby is four to five months old, you should be able to get a wrapper in the rear sweep. You may have to wash the sweep first, but make sure it is completely dry before you wrap it. The wrapper will probably come out at first, but you must persevere and replace it.

Later on, you can put the wrappers in the sides, perhaps when the cavy is about six or seven months old; you will need larger wrappers, one on each side. Try to include some of the frontal hair in the side wrappers, or you may prefer to put a small wrapper in the frontal itself.

The wrappers themselves should be quite small to start with, perhaps about one and a half, by three-quarters of an inch, but you will find that they need to be larger as your cavy, and its hair, grows.

Thin balsa wood is the best base for a wrapper; it is light and does not disintegrate it wet (as cardboard does). Strong kitchen roll is good for the wrapper itself, or even a cloth. Thin plastic, such as food bags, can be used over the actual wrapper to prevent wet getting through the cavy's coat, but plastic can also cause some condensation.

It is a good idea to ask an experienced fancier, at a show, to demonstrate how to set about brushing and fixing wrappers. Most Peruvian club members are willing to help newcomers and show them how they wrap their cavies – just the odd one or two regard it as a trade secret!

The diagram shows how to make up a wrapper and use it. The wrapper is secured by two elastic bands (in case one gets nibbled!). Whether to sellotape the fold or now is down to personal preference.

When you put wrappers in a cavy's coat, be sure it is comfortable and there is no strand of hair being pulled, or the cavy might chew it off. Sometimes you have a cavy who will not keep wrappers, no matter how hard you try, and some will not tolerate being brushed and groomed, twisting and jumping around when you attempt to groom them. Relegate these to the breeding pen.

PREPARING A WRAPPER

1. Place the balsa wood base on the paper wrapper.

2. Fold over the top of the paper.

3. Secure the flap with tape.

4. and 5. Fold lengthways into three.

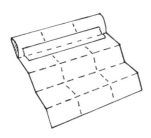

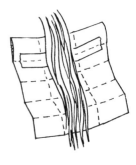

6. Concertina fold.

7. Open out, and place the fall of hair along the wrapper.

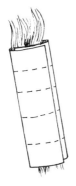

8. Fold over lengthways.

9. Re-fold concertina folds and secure with elastic band(s).

When you take your cavy to a show, you must have a stand that is similar to a little stool. It must be square, flat-topped, and several inches high. It must be covered with natural-coloured hessian (similar to that used for millers' sacks). No padding must be used under the hessian, and it should be firmly fixed to the board.

On arrival at the show, you will be issued with an 'ear label'. In the case of all longhaired breeds, this label must be firmly fixed to the top of your board, in one of the corners – NOT on the ear of your pig. If exhibiting more than one cavy and using the same board, make sure the correct label is on the board at the time the judge examines your exhibit.

As your cavy grows, so must the size of your board. Babies should be started off on a board approximately six inches square. The serious exhibitor should have three sizes of boards – six inches square, ten inches square, and 18 to 20 inches square. The board should be large enough to give a good outline of coat shape, but be a maximum of 20 inches square.

APPENDIX

BIBLIOGRAPHY AND WEBSITE LISTINGS

BOOKS

Introductory and children
All About Your Guinea Pig
Bradley Viner (Ringpress Books, 1997)
ISBN 1 86054 031 7

Getting To Know Your Guinea Pig
Gill Page (Interpet Publishing, 2000)
ISBN 1 90309 814 9

101 Facts About Guinea Pigs
Julia Barnes (Ringpress Books, 2001)
ISBN 1 86054 138 0

General information and care
Guinea Pigs: How To Care For Them, Feed Them, And Understand Them
Katrin Behrend (Barrons, 1997)
ISBN 0 81206 596 4

Pet Owner's Guide To The Guinea Pig
Chris Henwood (Ringpress Books, 1998)
ISBN 1 86054 110 0

The Guinea Pig: An Owner's Guide To A Happy Healthy Pet
Audrey Pavia (Howell Book House, 1997)
ISBN 0 87605 527 7

Breeding and showing
National Cavy Club Handbook 2003
Southern Cavy Club Handbook 2003
Available from National Cavy Club UK (see websites).

WEBSITES

National Cavy Club (UK)
http://www.geocities.com/nationalcavyclub/index.html

American Cavy Breeders Association
http://acbaonline.com

Southern Cavy Club
http://www.vivamiga.u-net.com

General information and care

Canny Cavies
http://www.oginet.com/Cavies/

Cavies Galore!
http://www.caviesgalore.com

Guinea Pig Care
http://www.guineapigs.info/sites.htm

Guinea Pig Compendium
http://www.aracnet.com/~seagull/Guineas/

The Pig Files
http://www.coldal.org/cavie.htm

Health and veterinary
Cavy Emergencies
http://cavyinfo.com/

Peter Gurney's Guinea Pig Medical Guide
www.oginet.com/pgurney/index.html

Online cavy magazines
Cavies Dot Com
www.cavies.com/

The Guinea Mag
http://www.angelfire.com/mi/csreidsma/guineamag.html